LIVING

BORDERLINE

A Mother's Memoir

LIVING BORDERLINE

A Mother's Memoir

Linda Burch

BALLEO Publishing, New York

This is a true story, told exactly as it occurred to the best of my memory. The names of people and places have been changed to protect privacy.

All rights reserved. Published in the United States by Balleo Publishing, New York.

ISBN 978-0-989709521

Library of Congress Control Number: 2015914815

Burch, Linda

Non-fiction

www.GrowingUpBorderline.com

Printed in the United States of America

First Edition

Dedication

In loving memory of my father and mother.

I hope you are smiling down at your granddaughter's progress.

I think motherhood is the noblest task of all because you cannot do it at your convenience or tailor it to suit your preferences. You have to be ready to give up everything when you take on this task: your time, restful nights, your hobbies, your pursuit of physical fitness, any beauty you may have had, and all of the private little pleasures you might have counted as a right, from late dinners and long soaks in the tub to weekend excursions and cycling trips. I'm not saying you can't have any of these things, but you have to be ready to let them all go if you're going to have children and put them first.

--Johann Christoph Arnold, <u>Endangered: Your Child in a Hostile World</u>

Contents

Preface

My daughter, Lisa, has been afflicted with borderline personality disorder, or BPD, for her entire life, but she didn't know it for a long time. Neither her doctors nor I knew it either because BPD is not usually diagnosed until adulthood. Yet, Lisa is living proof that symptoms of the disorder can appear in childhood, even infancy.

She and I struggled through the first eighteen years of her life as she suffered with learning and behavioral problems in school, severe temper tantrums and mood swings, anger outbursts, anxiety, pulling out her hair, bed-wetting, abnormal sleep patterns, poor impulse control, and troubled interpersonal relationships. Doctors, teachers, psychologists, and other specialists were all at a loss as to what was wrong and what to do about it. She was in and out of a labyrinth of psychiatric hospitals, residential treatment centers, and detention centers. She was given countless diagnoses and put on a myriad of different medications that were tried and abandoned. All the while, I fought with schools, insurance companies, the legal system, and the mental health care system to get the help my child needed.

These battles are all detailed in my previous book, *Growing up Borderline: A Mother's Memoir,* which chronicles our family's tumultuous lives until Lisa was finally diagnosed with borderline personality disorder at the age of eighteen. This book picks up Lisa's story from that point and describes the challenges and tribulations we faced and continue to face as Lisa contends with this disease as an adult.

Borderline personality disorder is an illness that irreparably changes the world for the ones plagued with it and for their families and friends, who don't know where to turn, how to help, what to do when they can't help, and how to keep going. This book is not intended to give you all the answers, but it will tell you what I did, what worked, and what didn't— for my daughter and me.

—Linda Burch

Introduction

Most people have never heard of borderline personality disorder, even when they may have it themselves. Borderline personality disorder, or BPD, is a devastating mental illness that has been shrouded in mis-information and myth. It has been one of the most feared, stigmatizing, and difficult-to-treat disorders and has one of the highest suicide rates, with up to ten per cent of patients committing suicide.

BPD centers on three core difficulties: the inability to manage emotions, impulsive behavior, and disturbed personal relationships. The symptoms include impulsivity, reckless behavior, severe mood changes, rage episodes, bodily self-harm, suicide attempts, chaotic relationships, and fear of abandonment. BPD can also be complicated by brief psychotic episodes.

Nearly ninety per cent of those with BPD are also diagnosed with one or more other major mental illnesses—called comorbid disorders—such as depression, bi-polar disorder, substance abuse, PTSD, anxiety disorders, ADHD, and eating disorders. In order to treat the BPD effectively, any comorbid disorders must be treated as well.

First described in the 1600's but not recognized by the medical community and defined until 1980, BPD affects over six million people in the United States. That makes BPD twice as common as schizophrenia and fifty percent more common than Alzheimer's disease. This also means that for every borderline, there are usually at least three non-borderlines (the BPD's parent, partner, child, friend, sibling, etc.) who are also affected.

Experts do not yet know what causes BPD, but studies of twins with BPD suggest that the condition may be inherited, with changes in certain parts of the brain. It is difficult to diagnose, not only because the condition's symptoms overlap with other mental illnesses, but because individual cases can vary greatly. For the condition to be diagnosed, a person must show at least <u>five</u> of the nine symptoms outlined in the Diagnostic and Statistical Manual of Mental Disorders (these are explained in the Appendix). My daughter had all nine, but there are 126 different possible combinations of symptoms!

Until the 1990's there was no treatment for BPD. Today, the recommended treatment is dialectical behavior therapy, which synthesizes cognitive behavioral therapy and Zen techniques. It has been proven to significantly reduce suicidality, self-injurious behaviors, substance abuse, and psychiatric hospitalizations. There are currently no medications approved by the FDA to treat BPD.

Chapter 1

What Happens in Vegas

I had no idea where my daughter was. The last time I heard from her was when she called me from the Houston bus station, informing me that she and a young man whose street name was Splash were going to Las Vegas. Lisa was eighteen and ostensibly an adult, but because of her emotional and mental disorders that included borderline personality disorder, her decision-making skills were no better than a child's.

She had been under the care of many different psychiatrists and psychologists since she was six years old, but none of them knew what was really wrong with her. She was diagnosed and medicated for illnesses ranging from ADHD to conduct disorder to fetal alcohol syndrome, yet her behaviors and symptoms got worse with age. Finally, my husband, Bill, and I felt that to keep her safe, we had to put her in a locked treatment center. When she was eighteen and legally an adult, she checked herself out and began living on the streets of Houston.

It was, ironically, when she turned eighteen and could legally refuse medical help that doctors were finally willing to diagnose her with borderline personality disorder. You see, although she had had the symptoms of this horrendous illness almost since birth, doctors had refused to call it what it was. One reason was that children's and adolescents' brains continued to develop until the late teens, and it was hoped that she would "grow out of" her problems. There was also great disinclination among psychiatric professionals to make the diagnosis of BPD in children and adolescents for fear that it would label them with one of the most feared, stigmatized, and difficult-to-treat disorders in psychiatry. Ignorance about mental illness leads some people to judge mental illness as a moral failing or a lack of willpower, rather than a biological chemical imbalance in the brain. The final reason was that there was no known treatment or cure for BPD anyhow, so why label someone with it?

As a legal adult, Lisa could go where she wanted and didn't have to be in a treatment center, so she chose to live on the streets with homeless teens. There she felt accepted and could do what she wanted to do.

I received collect phone calls from Lisa from New Orleans, Mississippi, El Paso, Phoenix, and Las Vegas during the first few months after she turned eighteen. Evidently, she and her friend Splash had stayed in New Orleans for a couple of days before continuing via Mississippi, El Paso, and Phoenix, to Las Vegas.

In Las Vegas, she and Splash went their separate ways. She had no money except for $20 that Splash gave her before he left. She barely had time to spend it, however, when she met Woody, a twenty-two-year-old professional boxer who was trying to make a living in the boxing capital of the world while staying with his mother in a Las Vegas suburb. Lisa moved in with them.

I hadn't heard from her for several days, when she called and said she and Woody needed to leave Las Vegas.

"Why do you need to leave?" I questioned.

"Because Woody's mom is getting tired of us living with her and eating her food."

"What are you going to do? Are you going to stay together with Woody?"

"Yes. He's really good to me, and we want to stay together. We are thinking about going to Phoenix, getting an apartment, and finding jobs. He doesn't want to stay in Las Vegas because there is too much criminal activity."

This was music to my ears. Lisa wanted to settle down. *Maybe she had hit bottom on the streets of Las Vegas and was ready to get back into the mainstream of life. I had to try to help her succeed.*

Before Lisa left Houston with Splash, she and I had gone to the local Social Security Office and filed an application for SSI. The Supplemental Security Income (SSI) program pays benefits to disabled adults and children who have limited income and resources.

The approval process was difficult and time-consuming, and the requirements were strict. However, after a thorough review of her finances and a comprehensive psychiatric examination by a State-appointed psychiatrist, who deemed her disabled mentally, she was approved and qualified for just over $500 a month. It was this money that I hoped could be used to get her started in an apartment. By being approved for SSI, she also became eligible for Medicaid, the national health program for people with low income and limited resources.

I flew to Phoenix, Arizona, on December 10, as soon as I finished giving final exams and turned in grades, to help Lisa and Woody find an apartment and get settled in.

After consulting with an apartment-finder agency, the three of us looked at a one-bedroom, one-bath apartment in a beautiful part of the city called Ahwatukee, between the Maricopa Freeway and Desert Foothills Estates. The grounds were tropically landscaped with water features and a duck pond—which Lisa loved—and the rent was an acceptable $475 per month.

Lisa and Woody signed a six-month lease, and I wrote a check for the first month's rent and the security deposit, which totaled $1,002. Then we were off to Target to buy furnishings for the space and some food for the kitchen. I spent the night in a local hotel and returned to Houston the next day.

I was in a great mood. I had missed out on many of the milestones that mothers of teenage girls experience while Lisa was in residential treatment. However, I had just been able to help my daughter in a very important rite of passage: getting settled in her very first apartment. She had an income of about $500 a month from SSI, and Woody would find a job, and she would see the wonderful life she could have in mainstream society.

Naively and with the hope that springs eternal in all mothers, I thought we were home free.

Chapter 2

Desert Debacle

On Christmas day, after having dinner with my parents, my husband, Bill, and I came home to a message on our answering machine from Lisa. She had called from a pay phone at the Grand Canyon.

In a voice cracking with emotion, she said Woody had been arrested and was being taken back to Las Vegas to jail on two outstanding warrants. She added that she had been robbed after Woody left and didn't want to stay in Phoenix by herself, so she was headed back to Las Vegas to stay with Woody's mom.

The next day I called the apartment manager and discovered that Lisa and Woody had been evicted for falsifying their application.

"What do you mean, they falsified their application? I was right there and helped them fill it out!" I nearly shouted into the phone.

7

The manager patiently explained that Woody had not divulged that there were warrants out for his arrest in Nevada. In addition, there had been reports of drug use in their apartment and a window had been broken. Furthermore, penalties for failure to fulfill the lease, broken window repair, and cancellation fees amounted to just over $1,000, which would be detailed in a final billing statement that I would receive.

I grabbed the nearest chair and sat down, my hand over my face in disbelief and astonishment. I was in mild shock and could do little else but stare straight ahead as Bill walked over and put his arms around me.

I sat silent for a moment until anger kicked in. I felt used and betrayed. I also felt foolish. I rescued Lisa because she had convinced me that she was ready to settle down and give up the uncertain and dangerous life of the streets. Now, seventeen days later, she was homeless again and back on the streets. She said she was going to stay with Woody's mom, but I doubted that his mom would allow that, if indeed Lisa was even telling me the truth about going there.

A week passed, and I didn't hear from Lisa. I really hadn't wanted to hear from her because I was still angry. However, she had never let this much time pass between calls.

My uneasiness finally got the best of me, and I called Woody's mom using a number I had saved on my caller ID.

Woody's mom said she had not seen Lisa since she and Woody left for Phoenix a month ago. She did confirm, though, that Woody was in jail. She gave me Woody's grandfather's and his brother's numbers to call. It was the same story there. Neither had seen Lisa.

Suddenly, my heart drummed fear against my ribcage. The emotional roller coaster of moving into her own place, coupled with Woody's arrest, and her subsequent eviction probably put her into a state of mind that was dangerous and life-threatening. I felt a tremendous amount of guilt for hoping she wouldn't call. *How could a mother do that?*

I felt I had to do something, so I called the Missing Persons Unit in Las Vegas. I told them no one had heard from Lisa in a week and that I felt her life was in danger because she was mentally ill and probably had no medication with her. They asked me to fax them documentation of her illness and a photograph, as well as any telephone numbers I could find. A detective would get back to me the next day, I was told.

I had difficulty sleeping, always afraid to go to sleep, fearing a 3 a.m. phone call telling me she had been found dead in an alley. *How was I going to let go?*

Previous conversations with mothers who had completely cut ties with their troubled children haunted me. They had to do it, they insisted. It was a matter of their own survival. They just couldn't take the roller coaster of fear, pain, and worry anymore. *Was I at that point?*

No, I knew I wasn't. I felt in my bones that God had given Lisa to me because he needed someone strong to be her mother. A friend once told me, "God never gives you more than you can handle—and you can handle more than most." I had been blessed with a husband more supportive, more generous, and more loving than I deserved, and with his strength I would continue trying to help my daughter.

I violated my own rule of not allowing cell phones in my English classroom at Houston Community College because I was so anxious to hear from the police. The call I received, however, was not from Missing Persons, but from my ex-husband, David, who is Lisa's adoptive father. We divorced when Lisa was eleven.

David had heard from Lisa. She was in the psychiatric ward of a hospital in Los Angeles and was being released after a three-day stay.

"How did she get there?" I asked in disbelief and relief.

"She said that she got a ride to California with a guy who abandoned her in San Bernadino. She didn't know anyone and was all alone and scared, so she called the police. She knew that if she told them she was suicidal, they would take her to a hospital."

"What is she going to do now?" I asked.

"The hospital won't release her until she has a place to go, so I bought her a plane ticket to Houston," he continued. The fact that he bought her a plane ticket to Houston, where I lived, instead of to Atlanta, where he lived, was not lost on me.

But Lisa didn't fly to Houston. After the hospital sent her to the airport in a cab, she changed her destination to Las Vegas. She called me from Woody's mom's home.

"Mom, I wanted to be near Woody, so I came to Las Vegas and will stay with his mom."

Since she had lied before about staying with Woody's mom, I insisted on speaking with the mom.

"She's not here. She's at work," Lisa was quick to reply.

There was nothing I could do. Once again, she had called to let me know she was safe, but I had no idea where she really was or what she was going to do. I tried to call Woody's mom a few times over the next few days, but I never got an answer.

The next time I heard from Lisa, she was crying and nearly incoherent. After I got her to calm down, I was able to understand that she had been beaten up on the streets of Las Vegas and this time REALLY wanted to come home. She wanted me to send her an airplane ticket as her dad had done when she was in Los Angeles.

"No way!" I shot back. "I am not spending all that money on a plane ticket so you can decide to go somewhere else. If you really want to come home, I will buy you a bus ticket."

"But, Mom! It takes three days to get to Houston from Las Vegas!" she whined.

"You went out there on a bus, and you can come back on a bus," I countered.

Three days later, she called from the Houston bus station to inform me that she was in town and would be going back to the Montrose area to live with her friends on the streets.

Later the same week, she phoned from Ben Taub Hospital. She had been hit by a car as she was crossing a street on foot and had been taken by ambulance to the hospital. The driver of the car had sped off.

She reported that she was bruised but okay and had no broken bones. However, her back was very sore, and the doctor had told her she could have serious back problems in the future as a result of her injuries. *How right he would turn out to be.*

Chapter 3

A Roof over Her Head

Since I had been left "holding the bag" in Arizona for thousands of dollars for an apartment that she and Woody had skipped out on, I had no desire to repeat that mistake. However, I needed to find a way to use her SSI payments of approximately $500 a month to get her off the streets by using that money to rent an apartment for her.

Bill and I contacted an attorney with the Employee Assistance Program, a service provided to us through our employer, Houston Community College. We needed advice about how to go about securing a place for her to live. The attorney advised us not to co-sign a lease because we could be held liable for anything that happened on the leased property. This meant that Lisa had to qualify for a lease based upon her income alone.

Unfortunately, most apartment complexes have very strict guidelines for minimum monthly income to qualify for an apartment. Most required a monthly income of twice the amount of rent, and I couldn't find an apartment anywhere in Houston that would accept Lisa's $500 income as a qualification.

The only options remaining were hotels that rented rooms weekly, and the only ones she had enough money to rent were in rundown parts of Houston. Nonetheless, tiring of the street life, she agreed to trade it for a roof over her head and a bed with a mattress.

Of course, I couldn't trust her with her SSI check, so I intercepted it each month and paid the motel weekly. There was nothing left for food, so she and her street friends spanged (begged) on street corners to get enough money for food. She would often collect up to $15 in three or four hours, enough for hamburgers and Coca Colas twice a day.

She had to be careful, she told me, about the locations where she chose to beg. Hardened street people who had been doing this for years had staked out the best intersections and would get violent with anyone who usurped their spots.

Her street friends began posing problems. The unwritten law of the street people states that if one of them secures a place to stay, the entire clan gets to stay, too. Although the motel had a strict policy of no more than two people to a room, and I had drilled this policy into Lisa's head, about seven or eight street friends sneaked into her room every night and slept on the floor. She insisted to me that she couldn't tell them no.

They made a complete mess in the motel room, of course, so it didn't take long for management to discover the fraud and kick her out. So, she moved on to another weekly arrangement at another budget motel. This occurred three more times during the next few months.

I continued to scour the classifieds for a more permanent place for Lisa—in her price range—that was farther from the street scene. I checked out a place near downtown near Montrose and Alabama Streets that looked like an old warehouse. Inside, it was divided lengthwise by a long hallway, and on either side were rooms, somewhat like a dormitory.

Each room was only about ten by ten feet with a door to a tiny bathroom on one wall. On the opposite wall was a cabinet about three feet wide with a hot plate and a tiny refrigerator. The rooms rented for $80 per week, with electricity and water paid. There were no phone jacks, and the only telephone in the building was a pay phone in the hallway.

This place was going to be more secure than the motels because the door to the outside of the building was locked every night at 10:00 p.m. This meant that the street people couldn't sneak in.

There was one room available, so I rented it in her name.

The next thing we did was go to the Texas Health and Services Commission office to sign her up for food assistance, or "food stamps." After a four-hour wait, she was interviewed and granted $60 per month for food.

This was not enough to feed someone even minimally for a month, but it helped. I taught her how to shop for low-cost items that she could prepare on her hot plate. I also showed her how to refrigerate leftovers and re-heat them. This place was a far cry from how I wanted my daughter to live, but it was a start. *And a step up from the streets.*

I kept careful records of Lisa's Planned Parenthood visits and made sure that she received her birth control (Depo-Provera) shot on schedule every three months. I also regularly drove her to appointments with her new psychiatrist, whom we had found through Medicaid. His office was located quite a distance across town, but we were fortunate to find someone who accepted Medicaid insurance.

The psychiatrist placed her on Depakote to mitigate her violent episodes and Zoloft to treat her depression and panic disorder. We filled the prescriptions at a Walgreen's near the building where she lived. I had no idea if she actually took her medication as prescribed or if she sold it or if she threw it down the toilet, but at least she had medication again. Beyond physically placing the bottles in her hands, there wasn't anything I could do to assure that she ingested the pills twice a day.

Lisa still hung around the street kids of Montrose during the day. She seemed to find the street life, with its so-called freedom, highly addicting. And, of course, when her street "family" discovered she had an SSI check and a room in which to live, they convinced her to let as many as five or six of them at a time go home with her.

It was about this time when someone new and different arrived in the Montrose area. He would prove to have a significant and lasting effect on many of the youth, and his name was Joe Sanders. Preacher Joe, as he was called, was an ordained minister who began holding Bible study services in a vacant lot in the heart of Montrose on Wednesday nights. He enticed the youth to his Bible study by offering free cookies and coffee.

Together with another mission group, his goal was to transition at-risk urban youth away from the streets by placing them into shelters, drug and alcohol rehabilitation programs, maternity and transitional living homes, or reuniting them with their families.

Preacher Joe became Lisa's mentor and best friend. She attended Street Church every week and began reading the Bible regularly. From the four kids that attended on the first night of Street Church, the ministry quickly grew to as many as 75 youths who came to listen to Preacher Joe and eat cookies every Wednesday night.

Lisa now had 75 new, homeless, troubled friends.

Chapter 4

Motel Surfing

By early June of 2001 when she was nineteen, Lisa had been evicted from Alabama House for allowing too many people to live there with her and her boyfriend Chris. I decided to clean up her apartment so that I could get the deposit back, but when I entered the tiny space, I nearly gagged.

The filth and trash strewn everywhere were a foot deep. You couldn't see the floor. I had to work my way in by throwing fast-food bags with half-eaten food, half-filled soft drink cups, cigarette butts, empty cans, dirty clothes, and old magazines into trash bags—twelve of them. I had to throw away all of her pots and plates and utensils because they were so nasty with caked-on food and strange things growing on them.

She hadn't cleaned or thrown anything away or washed any clothes since she moved in, and with who-knows-how-many street kids staying there every night, trash built up fast.

To add insult to injury, in spite of all my efforts at cleaning, I never got my deposit back.

She and Chris moved into a motel again, and I scoured the ads once more to find a place for her to live. One of the ads mentioned government-assisted programs that help people on SSI or Disability get affordable housing. Some apartment complexes receive money from the federal government if they rent units at a reduced rate to disabled tenants who would not ordinarily qualify because of low income.

One such apartment complex was located in a middle-class area of Houston with shops and restaurants. Garden Place Apartments were miles from the downtown area and the street kids—too far for them to walk for a place to sleep! It was a gated community (another plus) and the units were lovely.

Rents were normally in the $800-$900 per month range, but Lisa, because of her disabilities, would pay $495, plus electricity. By now, her SSI income had increased to $525 per month, and it seemed like a very good deal. *We'd been given another chance.*

Unfortunately, Preacher Joe asked Lisa if he could visit her shortly after she moved in. She told him the gate keypad code, so he could drive onto the property. When he arrived in his beat-up old van, the doors opened, and out came four of the homeless young adults in his street ministry. Joe begged

Lisa to let them stay with her, adding the guilt trip of, "You have a place to stay, and they don't."

Lisa said they could stay.

I didn't know about it for about a week. When I discovered what was happening, I told everyone except Lisa and Chris to leave. I explained that her rental agreement was for only two persons and that she could be evicted if the others stayed.

The street friends politely left without any problems, and I helped Lisa clean up the mess of dirty dishes, dirty clothes, and trash that had accumulated in a week. Of course, when I asked her why she had agreed to let them stay, her only response was, "Preacher Joe asked me to, and I felt bad for them."

My self-pity kicked in and I said, "What about feeling bad for ME and all I do for you? I'm trying to help you live a decent life, and you give me obstacles every step of the way."

At that point, she got angry, turned on her heel, and walked away.

Six weeks later, Lisa received a letter from the complex manager:

"You are to vacate said premises within three days of receipt of this letter. Your right to occupy the leased premises is hereby terminated as a result of criminal activity, continual disruptive behavior, and numerous resident complaints."

She had been living in a far nicer place than she had any right to expect, and she blew it. Again.

During the next few months Lisa was in and out of motels. At one point, I had found a garage apartment for her in an area of town called the Heights. It was accurately called a "garage" apartment in that it was a 16 foot by 20 foot detached garage that the owner had turned into a living space (and I use the term loosely) by adding plumbing and electricity.

By this time, Lisa had a different boyfriend, Eric, and the two of them managed to clog the plumbing so badly that neighbors complained of the smell. As a result, the Health Department investigated and ended up condemning the unit. It was back to dumpy motels for them.

During this period of moving from one motel to the other, Lisa found an abandoned puppy on the streets and took it in. The puppy, named Lady, became her constant companion. She told me that it was now easier to get people to give her money on the street corners with Lady at her side. There was something about a dog that made people more compassionate and generous.

One evening I had to make a phone call to Lisa that no one ever wants to make. I had to tell her that my daddy—Lisa's grandpa—had died. It was a sudden death from a heart attack, so all of us were somewhat in a state of shock. For Lisa and for borderlines in general, feelings of grief are magnified ten-fold with the death of a close family member, and abandonment responses are triggered.

As I had feared, Lisa reacted to his death very badly. She seemed to be in a state of anger and depression, and the day before the funeral she tried to ingest an entire bottle of her psychiatric meds. Eric grabbed her wrist before she could empty the bottle into her mouth. She struggled so violently that she fractured her wrist. She went to the funeral with her arm in a cast, and I checked her into the psychiatric hospital the next day. She only remained in the hospital a few days before being deemed stable and released.

She re-joined Eric in their hotel room. Although she still expressed sadness that she didn't know how to deal with, one thing I said may have helped more than anything. I reminded her that now her grandpa would be in heaven with Granny and PawPaw (her dad's parents), and they would be so happy to see each other. They were probably playing dominoes and watching television together. Somehow the visual of that scenario worked to ease her confusion and grief.

A few weeks later, she called me from the City Jail, wailing hysterically that she had been picked up on an outstanding warrant for her arrest.

What now?

After some digging, I discovered that she had lost her State-issued identification card some months earlier. Whoever found it (or stole it) had used it to stiff a cab driver for a large fare. The driver took Lisa's name off the ID and reported it to the police.

Lisa knew that I wouldn't bail her out of jail if she were ever arrested; however, this time she was innocent. *Sort of. She was still guilty of carelessness.*

I contacted a bonding company and got her out of jail the next day at a cost of $750 for the bond. The case was dismissed two months later.

I kept the business card from the bail bondsman. I had a feeling I would need it again in the future.

Chapter 5

One More Try

Eric had stuck with Lisa for over six months, and he seemed to be a stabilizing influence on her. He was an orphan and had been in and out of foster homes all his life. When he turned eighteen, he aged out of the system and began living on the streets, where he met Lisa. Eric and Lisa had now been living in the same motel unit for two months without being asked to leave, and Eric was not shy about telling their street friends that they could not stay with Lisa and him.

One day, Lisa and Eric came to me and said, "Mom, we think we have grown up and are ready to take responsibility for our lives. Will you help us find an apartment again?"

After this period of relatively good behavior, I, too felt it was time to get them into an apartment again, but unless I signed the lease, there wasn't one they qualified for. Bill and I discussed the situation and agreed that we would try to be their landlords. We purchased a 750-square-foot studio townhome for $26,500 about ten minutes from our home.

It was not quite a fixer-upper, but it was close. I didn't want to spend a lot of money on a townhome or condo in case this idea didn't pan out. We replaced the countertop in the bathroom, shampooed the carpets, and gave the place a general cleaning to make it look acceptable.

Lisa, Eric, and Lady moved in during the last week of May, 2002. Since leaving the treatment center shortly after her eighteenth birthday in 2000, she had been living on the streets or in dirty motels for a year and nine months. She was three months shy of her twentieth birthday.

Being her landlord was going to bring an entirely new set of problems and issues, but if it would keep her off the streets, Bill and I were willing to try.

Being Lisa's landlord was not going to be easy, as I soon discovered. I don't think I ever believed that it would be smooth sailing, but I had hoped that since I was her landlord, we could avoid the frequent evictions. Unfortunately, I had forgotten about something called the homeowner's association.

Almost immediately after Lisa moved in, I began receiving notices two or three times a month of townhome association rule violations. Each notice was sent by certified mail, so in addition to any fines, I had to pay the $10 cost for the certified letter.

At first, the violations were all related to Lisa's mixed-breed dog, Lady. Although I had explained the regulations to her, I received notice after notice of violations: the dog relieved herself on the grass; the dog was running around without a leash; the dog was in the pool area; the dog relieved herself in the pool area, etc.

Lisa just couldn't—or wouldn't—abide by the rules. I think she understood them; she was just too lazy. It was easier to let Lady out of the house until she did her business in the common areas and then let her back in. After all, it wasn't Lisa who was paying the fines—I was. Theoretically, I took the money from her SSI allotment, but after paying for taxes, maintenance, electricity, television, and a phone for her unit, there wasn't any money left for paying fines. It came out of my pocket. In addition, Lisa refused to take responsibility and denied the charges, insisting that whoever was complaining to the board was lying because they didn't like her.

Another association bylaw that she just couldn't follow was the restriction on what time and which days trash was to be put outside the gated patio for pickup. She put her trash bags out whenever she thought of it. This was actually an improvement over what she used to do when she first moved in: not empty her trash cans at all and just allow the garbage to overflow onto the floor.

We had a serious discussion about these problems.

"Lisa, if you can't follow the rules, you are going to have to pay your own fines. You have to get a job. Maybe then you will learn the value of what these fines are costing."

"But, Mom," she wailed. "If I get a job, then I will lose my SSI and there won't be any money to pay my rent."

I had a response ready. "Lisa, your SSI only goes down for every dollar you earn, so if you only make $300 per month, you will still get some SSI. Plus, you need to start learning to support yourself and not depend on your SSI for income. Despite your disabilities, there are many jobs that you could possibly do, and it would make you feel so much better about yourself."

She didn't resist any harder. I think she accepted the idea of a job as something she needed. We discussed the type of work that she should seek, keeping in mind her psychological problems, her mathematics disability, and the fact that she was a high school dropout. Furthermore, she didn't have a car, so she needed to work nearby or on a bus route.

The next day she called me on the phone, bursting with excitement about being hired at the McDonald's restaurant that was only one block from her house. I was delighted and told her I was very proud of her efforts.

Chapter 6

Can I Have Fries with That?

It was Thursday, October 10, 2002, the day before she was to begin training for the job at McDonalds at 8:00 a.m. Eric reported to me that Lisa had become nervous, agitated, and anxious about beginning a new job. I tried to talk to her about her feelings and how normal they were for anyone beginning a new job, but she didn't seem able to express her emotions. She didn't even want to talk about them.

The next morning, I went to work as usual, and when I checked my phone messages between classes, I had a message from Eric, asking me if I had seen Lisa. My stomach plummeted as I called him back. He said she must have left their townhome in the very early morning hours because when he awoke at 7 a.m., she was gone.

When I arrived home, I discovered that she had broken two windows to enter my house and then had rifled through my bedroom looking for cash. *Did I think for a second that it was a random burglar and not Lisa? No.*

Lisa finally returned to her townhome the next day, after spending the previous 24+ hours with "friends" in the Montrose area. She admitted to breaking into my home, but told me she didn't take anything. She said she didn't know why she had done it but that she was sorry and would pay for the windows. She seemed very relieved that she had missed her orientation and training at McDonald's.

Later that day, we talked about her response to a new job—how scared and nervous she must have been—and the pressure she felt. I tried to make her understand that she should just do her best, and if she doesn't like the job or if she gets fired, that's okay. She then called McDonald's and told them she was sick. They asked her to come the following Monday for training, which she agreed to do.

Lisa did go to McDonald's the following Monday for two days of training and seemed to enjoy it. However, on the third day, they assigned her to the drive-through window to "test" her ability to perform there. She became very nervous as she was told she had to process the customers within ninety seconds—from the time they place their orders until they received their orders and their change. Because of her math disability, she had great difficulty making change, and that was compounded by having to take orders at the same time.

At the end of the shift, which was the busy 11 to 2 lunch shift, she was two dollars short in her cash drawer. It was unclear as to whether Lisa just chose not to return or if they asked her not to return; either way, she was finished working at McDonald's.

I asked her why she had been placed in the high-stress cashier job and not in the kitchen. She replied that she had told her supervisor on the first day that she has borderline personality disorder and was prone to emotional outbursts. Her supervisor had said, "Well, we won't let you cook in the kitchen then because you might throw hot grease on somebody if you got mad at them."

Approximately ten days later, Bill and I discovered that his laptop computer was missing. It didn't even belong to us; it was on loan from the college we both worked for, so we were particularly upset. I confronted Lisa. At first she denied knowing anything, but finally, after I promised not to be angry, she admitted selling it to a pawn shop.

Since the computer belonged to the college, I was desperate to get it back, so Lisa and I went to the pawn shop together. The shop clerk was not helpful at all, although it had to have been very clear to him when she brought it in that the computer had been stolen because of all the password protection and college identifying tags.

He said that since there was no police report, he would not give it to us even though we offered to return the forty dollars Lisa had received for it. He said that we would have to wait twenty days and then would have to buy it back at the selling price. He did agree to hold it for us, but we had to pay $150 to get it back when we returned in twenty days.

The next day, I received a notice from the bank that her account was overdrawn. This is when I discovered that a check was missing from Lisa's checkbook, which I keep and administer. Lisa had written a check to Gerland's grocery store for $77 although she only had $8 in her account. The bank paid the check but charged the account $30 for the overdraft. I transferred money from my personal account into hers to cover the overdraft and penalty.

Upon confrontation, she admitted to taking the check but added that she only bought groceries with it, as if that made her theft acceptable. She also insisted that it was "her" money. She just couldn't seem to grasp the notions that she can't just take things from my home even if she thinks they belong to her and that she can't just write a check without knowing how much money is in the account. In her mind, her actions were justified because she "needed the money."

Chapter 7

Townhome Troubles

The headaches and financial costs of being Lisa's landlord continued. We averaged two to three violation letters and fines per month. Some were legitimate transgressions, but many seemed excessive. Lisa vehemently denied many of the violations and insisted that someone "had it in for her" and was watching her.

Each transgression amounted to a fine that began at $25 and doubled each time the same violation occurred. Bill and I paid most of the fines, the ones for acts we figured that Lisa probably committed and that were clear violations of the bylaws: did not pick up after dog, broken window in unit, trash left at the pool, music too loud at pool, excessive noise coming from unit.

There were many, however, that we felt were ridiculous, such as "people coming and going at all hours, sitting on cars in the parking lot, took trash to the dumpster in a grocery cart." Bill and I were pretty sure that Lisa had indeed committed these acts, but we perused the bylaws from top to bottom and could not find any reference to them as violations. So, in a polite letter, we refused to pay.

I was beginning to agree with Lisa that she was being singled out because "someone" didn't want her living there, and I had a suspicion as to who it was. A lady who only identified herself as Dee, had begun calling me regularly to "report" what she had observed happening at Lisa's unit. These calls came late at night, usually around midnight when we had already gone to bed. In one call, she self-righteously announced to me that some black people had just left Lisa's townhome. I was a bit stunned, but politely asked her, "Is that against regulations—to have black people visit?" She responded, "No, but I just thought you should know."

Another time she called and said that a homeless person who lingers on a nearby street corner had come out of Lisa's apartment. On yet another occasion late at night, she called to inform me that Lisa was talking to a black man in the parking lot and was probably buying drugs from him.

I don't always behave well when someone awakens me in the middle of the night, and I responded angrily, "What business is it of yours? Why are you up at 1 a.m. spying on my daughter? It is none of your business who comes and goes from her unit. Please don't call me again."

She didn't call me again, but soon afterward, we received a letter from the attorneys retained by the townhome association to enforce the bylaws, which stated, "Please be advised that if you have not corrected the above-mentioned violations within ten days of this letter, the association has directed us to file suit against you seeking civil damages of up to $200.00 per day and/or a court order directing you to comply. You will, if the association prevails, be charged all costs and attorney fees associated with this matter, which can represent a substantial expense. Due to your failure to comply with the bylaws prior to this firm's involvement, please forward a check made payable to the association in the amount of $210."

It was a threat that was meant to scare us.

Bill and I consulted an attorney from Legal Access that had been recommended by the Employee Assistance Program associated with Houston Community College. We told him about the huge number of violation notices and that we were sure Lisa was guilty of some of them; however, we also felt that she was being harassed.

The attorney replied that because Lisa has been officially designated as disabled according to State and Federal guidelines, she has protection under the Americans with Disabilities Act for mental illness. In addition, Federal fair housing laws may have been violated. He recommended that we NOT pay the $210 to the association because they have no proof of the assertions. In addition, he offered to write a threatening letter of his own, asking them to stop harassing and fining us. Legal Access allows one letter without charge, and thereafter the fee is $200 per letter. After a short discussion, we all agreed to request a hearing of the association's board of directors first and see what happens there.

What a shock I received when I walked into the board meeting room two weeks later and discovered that the lady who had made those calls to me in the middle of the night was the chair of the homeowner's association board of directors. I had angered the dragon lady of the board.

The dragon lady was ready for us. Sitting next to her were the association's attorney, the manager, assistant manager, and the other four board members. I decided to let Bill do most of the talking because he is able to keep his cool better than I can, especially when I am irritated. I knew this was going to be a contentious meeting, and once again, it was David (us) vs. Goliath (the attorney, managers, and board). It reminded me of when we went up against the school district and its cadre of lawyers years earlier.

Bill opened by expressing our willingness to work with them to make sure that all bylaws were obeyed. "We are accepting responsibility for any legitimate violations," he continued, "but we believe that many of them are false and that Lisa is being unfairly targeted."

He then gave the example of the fine assessed for having an overweight dog. "Lady, Lisa's dog, at her last visit to the vet, was about fifty pounds. We are aware of several other dogs in the complex that are even heavier than Lady, but when we asked their owners if they had received any fines, they stated that they had not."

At that point I just couldn't contain myself, and I blurted, "Do you have any proof of any of the violations?"

"What kind of proof?" one of the board members asked.

"Anything that would document the violation, such as photographs, specific times and dates."

I could hear the pitch of my voice rising, as I continued. "None of the violation notices give any detail. They just say, 'Dog was without leash' or 'Dog was barking.' I'd like to know the name of the person who reported the violations."

The dragon lady interrupted and said, "We will not give you that information."

I knew at that moment that she was the person reporting violations to the management company. She had absolutely no accountability to anyone. All she had to do was instruct the management company to write a letter.. Then the management company would instruct their attorney to write a letter. Later I would learn from Lisa that dragon lady's townhome was directly across the parking lot from Lisa's and that she often sat in her window, watching Lisa's activities.

I was about to open my mouth again when Bill tugged at my shirt and spoke instead.

"As you may know, Lisa has a number of emotional and cognitive disabilities, and we are asking your patience as she learns the bylaws of the organization."

As soon as we mentioned the word "disability," the attorney spoke up. "We will need documentation of her disability and a statement from a veterinarian that her dog weighs 50 pounds or less, which is required in the bylaws."

I was ready for that. I produced the statement from the Social Security Administration recognizing Lisa as having a disability and a statement from Lady's veterinarian showing her weight as 50.0 pounds, the limit as stated in the bylaws.

As we prepared to leave the meeting, Bill continued, "To be specific, we deny most of the charges and allegations, and we believe that Lisa is being badgered by people who don't want her in the townhome community. We would like the harassing fines stopped."

Well, of course, the letters and fines didn't stop. But we had had an impact. After that meeting most of the violations mentioned a time and date. However, by the time we received the notice, the violation was over two weeks old, and who can remember what they were doing at a specific time two weeks earlier?

Now that we had specific dates on the violations, though, we could sometimes verify if Lisa had indeed broken a bylaw. For example, on one occasion we received two notices, one for each of two days that this violation allegedly occurred: "It was reported that on Sunday, January 18, you were out riding the scooter with the dog running loose. All pets must be on a leash at all times." The fines totaled $150.

We politely wrote to the management company. "On the dates in question, our tenant was out of town, and her dog was staying with us. Therefore, neither of the two violations could have been committed by our tenant. Furthermore, neither our tenant nor any of her acquaintances own a scooter. Please remove the fines totaling $150 from our account."

After several weeks, we finally received a response that stated the violation had been issued in error due to mistaken identity. Finally, we won one!

Another result of the meeting was that dragon lady could now be seen walking the property with a camera around her neck. She began snapping photos of every person who visited Lisa and their license plates. One day, she went too far.

Lisa called me in severe distress. She had slit her wrists very deeply, and a friend had already called 911. I drove like a maniac and actually arrived before the two EMTs and a policeman did. While the EMTs were treating Lisa in the ambulance, I was holding her hand, and the policeman was documenting the incident. Suddenly, dragon lady appeared and began snapping pictures with her camera.

When Lisa saw dragon lady, she became even more agitated and cried out, "I don't want my picture taken like this!" The EMTs continued to administer aid to Lisa, and one of them said, "That woman needs to leave because she is escalating the problem." I was apprehensive about Lisa's physical health as well as her state of mind, so I screamed hysterically at the top of my lungs, "You need to leave NOW!" The dragon lady's response to me was an obscene gesture with her middle finger.

One of the EMTs then gave her a threatening glance, and she slowly backed off. Or so we thought. She circled the building, returned from the opposite side, and continued to snap photos of the outside of the ambulance, the last one being of me as I stepped out. At this point, the policeman began to walk toward her, and she hurried behind a fence. A minute or so passed, and I saw her peering around the corner of the fence with her camera still in hand.

In addition to my concern for Lisa, I was livid. I immediately wrote a letter to the management and board of directors detailing what had happened, complete with names of the EMTs and policeman who were witnesses. I concluded in the letter:

"This lady has stalked my daughter, her visitors, her roommate, and her pet. Her most recent actions constitute a blatant invasion of privacy as well as disability harassment. According to my daughter's psychiatrist, these stressors can trigger my daughter's mental disorder, which can have tragic consequences. As a mother, I am concerned about the health and well-being of my daughter. As a homeowner, I am concerned that such continuing harassment will potentially place the townhome association in liability."

It was a thinly veiled threat against the association and dragon lady personally, and I hoped it would cause the rest of the board, and perhaps their attorney, to pressure her to back off.

Chapter 8

Two Steps Forward...

Along with the struggles that came with her borderline personality disorder, there were some positive things happening in Lisa's life. Three weeks before her twenty-first birthday, she decided that she wanted to go back to high school and complete the one credit she needed to obtain her high school diploma. In Texas, students who have dropped out of school are eligible to re-enroll until September first of the year they turn 21.

Of course, it wasn't quite as easy as it sounds. I called the special education office and asked how to proceed. I was referred to the campus instructional specialist who advised that two things needed to be done. First, I had to call the school district registrar and register Lisa for school. Next, the instructional specialist would convene an ARD. *Here we go again with the ARDs!*

An ARD, or Admission, Review, and Dismissal, meeting is necessary, according to Texas law, to create a comprehensive document that explains the individualized education program process for a student in a special education program.

Since classes for the semester had already begun, no time was wasted. A few days later, an ARD was convened, during which the registrar confirmed that, after interpreting her transcript, Lisa was only one credit shy of her diploma if she graduated under an individualized education plan. Under a regular plan, she would need ten credits. The special education director (a new one—not the one from a few years ago when we battled the school district) declared that Lisa would need another individual assessment confirming her special education eligibility because she had been out of school for three years. The testing would begin the next day and be completed within a week.

Because Lisa was not yet 21 years of age, Bill and I participated in the planning and process. As soon as she turned 21, which was in ten days, she would be considered an adult, and all communication would flow directly to and from her.

The individual assessment was completed within the week, and another ARD was convened immediately to discuss the results. The testing concluded that Lisa continued to meet eligibility requirements for the emotional disturbance condition and that she would benefit from a structured program with an emphasis on vocational/employability skills. Her IQ was estimated to be approximately 85.

Behavior and academic goals were set, and it was decided that Lisa would have two classes, mathematics and vocational training, both with experienced special education teachers. Five days before her twenty-first birthday, Lisa became a senior in high school again.

She loved her school experience this time, attended regularly, and thrived on the individualized attention. She had one classmate in her math class and two in her vocational class. Her math goals were simple: balance a checkbook using a calculator, set up a household budget, and understand cost effective shopping. She particularly enjoyed the last one because she, her classmate, and her teacher made trips to grocery stores, pharmacies, and Target to "comparison shop." She also learned functional skills by collecting apartment rent data to compare and evaluate cost, size, location, amenities, and lease restrictions.

There were probably many reasons why she suddenly became a good student. She was older and more mature, enjoyed the classes and teachers, felt independent, and had a clear goal of graduation. Whatever the case, she successfully completed both classes with grades of A, and at the age of 21, walked down the aisle of the school district coliseum to graduate and accept her diploma from the superintendent of schools.

We were all there to cheer her on. In addition to me, there was Bill, Brian, her boyfriend Eric, and Lisa's dad, who drove down from Georgia. *It was a big victory for all of us, but especially for Lisa.*

The next year, when Lisa was 22, Bill and I received a notice from our church that their records indicated Lisa had not been confirmed. In the Roman Catholic Church, young men and women traditionally receive the Sacrament of Confirmation at the age of discretion, typically around sixteen years of age. When Lisa was sixteen, she was in Six Meadows Treatment Center.

Despite the fact that Lisa had not attended Mass regularly in many years, the idea of being confirmed in the church really appealed to her. She was eager to begin the process, which consisted of five preparation sessions and twenty-four service hours. I contacted the adult education director and explained Lisa's mental and emotional disabilities, adding that this was something Lisa really wanted to do.

The director came up with a plan for Lisa to attend a discussion group for adults with cognitive disabilities that met every Monday night. After three months of meetings, she would be accepted as a confirmation candidate.

Lisa eagerly anticipated and enjoyed these meetings. She was one of the highest functioning people in the class, as most of them were severely learning disabled. Just as she had thrived in her early high school years helping the disabled students, she was confident and content in the environment. Just as promised, with her brother at her side as her sponsor, she received the Sacrament of Confirmation from the diocesan bishop three months later. *Again, another triumph!*

Chapter 9

...Two Steps Back

Intermingled among Lisa's successes was a series of borderline episodes. One morning she called me in a panicked emotional state. She was crying and seemed to be paranoid, depressed, and volatile.

"Mom, Eric has been seeing other girls. I know he has been unfaithful to me. He doesn't love me anymore!" she screamed into the phone, barely coherent. "It's all because of my weight." Partly because of the medication she was taking, her weight had ballooned to over 200 pounds.

Eric took the phone, and in tears, asked me for help. She was screaming outlandish accusations at him, he said, accusing him of being unfaithful to her.

He put Lisa back on the phone, and she then admitted that she had abruptly stopped taking her psych medications about a week earlier, when her prescriptions ran out. She also didn't keep her psychiatrist appointment to refill her meds. Her reason was that she didn't want to be put back on Depakote. She blamed the Depakote for the 75 pounds she gained over the previous nine months, so she abruptly stopped ALL her medication, including the anti-depressants.

She went on, "That doctor is so stupid. He never takes a blood test to see if I'm taking the right dose. At Six Meadows they took blood tests every month to make sure I wasn't taking too much or too little. This doctor has never taken a blood test. He doesn't know what he is doing. It's not working anyway!"

Depakote is classified as a mood stabilizer and works by increasing a calming chemical in the brain called GABA, which quietens overactive nerve cells. Two of its side effects are weight gain and liver damage, and yes, she was correct that blood levels should be monitored by blood tests monthly.

Unfortunately, many people with mental illnesses often stop taking their medication, often become sicker, and then can hurt themselves or others. They stop taking their pills for any of a number of reasons, including the ones Lisa used: side effects they didn't like or they felt the medication wasn't working.

My biggest challenge when she would call me out-of-the-blue in an emotionally-charged state like this one was to avoid being drawn into her drama and to stay calm. My first impulse was to scream back at her, "Why did you stop taking your meds? Don't you know that suddenly stopping such powerful medication can cause serious problems? What a stupid thing to do!"

Fortunately for me, her ranting went on so long that I had time to compose myself and prepare a rational response. I took a deep breath and told her, "Sweetheart, refusing to take a medication that doesn't work is understandable. Everyone has felt that way, but the trick is getting through the medication that doesn't work to find the one that does, and going off all medication is not the way to do this. We need to work with the doctor to find something better."

I stopped what I was doing and drove over to her townhome with some of her pills that I kept at home for just this type of incident. I called her psychiatrist and made an appointment for the next day to refill her medication. I drove her there myself and talked with the doctor about possible substitutes for the Depakote. He changed her prescription to Seroquel, a drug that treats mood disorders and also has anti-depressant properties. It was a good change; she still takes it every day.

Chapter 10

Downward Spiral

When Lisa was twenty-four, Eric made a decision to leave. He and Lisa had been attending Street Church with Preacher Joe every Wednesday night since they first met him years ago when Lisa was still living on the streets. Now, don't get me wrong; it wasn't solely because they had suddenly found God in their lives. Street Church on Wednesday nights in Montrose was where many charitable organizations brought food, clothing, and other items that had been donated for the needy. Lisa and Eric brought home some of all of it.

Nonetheless, the religious part of it must have taken hold because Eric decided he wanted to go to Faith Ministries in Dallas to study and work at their mission there "to re-connect with God and atone for all the bad things he had done in his life."

Lisa, of course, couldn't handle this perceived abandonment, though Eric assured her it would be only a year and then he would be back. To a borderline and to a two-year-old, a year is forever.

She became severely depressed and neglected personal hygiene and housekeeping. She was basically living in filth. You had to step over piles of dog poop on the patio to approach her front door. Trash bins were overflowing, and week-old food was caked onto dishes piled high in the sink and scattered on the floor. I didn't know how to motivate her to maintain even a minimum of cleanliness. I kept her pills and dispensed them daily because I was afraid that in her depression she might swallow the entire bottle.

I was keeping an eye on what had first looked like an insect bite on the tip of her pointer finger. It became reddish-black and puffy, with a whitish substance oozing from it, so I drove her to the emergency room. After examining her and taking blood, the hospital admitted her. She had developed a severe staph infection. For the first few days, she was resistant to the antibiotics she was given, and I began to be concerned that it might be one of the drug-resistant strains. After three days, however, they zeroed in on the correct treatment and her response was immediate. With the ubiquitous problem of drug-resistant bacteria roaming around in hospitals, the last thing the hospital wanted was someone with a staph infection, so they discharged her as soon as they could.

While she was in the hospital, I hired someone to clean her townhome from top to bottom. Not only did it desperately need de-cluttering and organizing, I wanted to disinfect it and eliminate any source of the staph infection.

Life went more smoothly—for her and thus for me—when she returned home. Her brother, Brian, was getting married soon, and she had been asked to be a bridesmaid by Brian's fiancée. As her finger healed, we shopped for her bridesmaid's dress and shoes, as well as the dress I would wear as mother of the groom. It got her mind away from Eric and her feelings of abandonment.

Eric returned to Houston via bus so that he could attend Lisa's brother's wedding. During the three days that he was here, he tried to convince her to join the ministry and move to Dallas to be near him. She was conflicted because she wanted to be with him, but she was afraid to leave Houston and be so far away from me. She told him that she would have to think about it, so Eric returned to Dallas, alone.

Over the next few weeks, Lisa confessed to me that she was afraid to be alone (a common borderline trait), so she had been allowing a string of people she knew from the streets to live with her. It didn't take long for the townhome association to begin sending me warning letters again that said "unsavory people are going in and out at all hours of the night."

A month after he left, Eric returned to Houston to attend the funeral of a friend. He stayed with Lisa, and as he was about to return to Dallas, Lisa informed me that she was going to move to Dallas and live in the mission's "women's home" located about fifteen minutes away from Eric's residence.

She told me Eric had called his pastor and asked if Lisa could join him in Dallas. The pastor replied that Lisa could come as soon as there was an opening in the women's residence. Eric decided to remain in Houston until he could bring Lisa back with him.

About ten days passed, and there was still no available room in the women's residence, so his pastor told Eric to go ahead and bring Lisa back to Dallas with him, and she could stay in the pastor's home until something became available. In the meantime, she could help the pastor's wife maintain their residence. *Really? She couldn't even keep her own place maintained.*

Nonetheless, Lisa packed up her car, and she and Eric drove to Dallas, spending the night with the pastor and his wife. At breakfast the next day, Lisa was told by the pastor's wife that after a year of training, she and Eric could marry and jointly run their own mission. The prospect thrilled Lisa.

I don't know if Lisa misunderstood, or if she did something to upset the pastor's wife, or what exactly happened, but later that same day around six o'clock, Eric phoned me and said that Lisa was on her way home because she had just been told by the pastor that there wouldn't be an opening in the women's home for her. The pastor went on to tell her that she could only learn to really know God if she spent time away from Eric, so the pastor would be sending her to the church's New York ministry.

According to Eric, Lisa became hysterical about the changed plans and immediately began the drive back to Houston around midnight, alone. She had taken a sedative because she was so upset and promptly fell asleep at the wheel. She was spotted swerving on the highway by a state trooper, who advised her to stop and rest in a motel before traveling on. Lisa, however, had no money, so she asked the motel manager if I could give him my credit card number over the phone. He refused, so Lisa continued toward Houston, arriving around 4 a.m.

At this point, her emotional health deteriorated rapidly, and a three-week period of a sequence of crises occurred. One warm summer Saturday evening in August, she and her friend Troya drove to a house in a questionable neighborhood in northeast Houston. Troya knew the people who lived there, but they weren't at home. The two men who were visiting the home invited Troya and Lisa in, but suddenly Troya walked out of the house, leaving Lisa there, and drove off in Lisa's car.

Lisa felt uncomfortable with the two strangers, so she went into the bathroom and locked the door. In just minutes, one of the men forced the door open and raped her in the bathroom, while the other held the bathroom door closed. When he was finished, the two men returned to the living room to watch television, and Lisa was able to run out the back door. Stunned and disheveled, she ran for blocks until she saw a police car. She told her story to the policemen and led them to the house, where they arrested the rapist.

She was taken to a hospital where a sexual assault exam was performed by compassionate and supportive staff. Tearing and bruising and the presence of semen in the vaginal area, plus bruises on her body where the assailant had held her down, confirmed her assault. The physical evidence, which included her clothes, was made available to the police with her permission.

Following a statement to the police, Lisa received the "morning after" emergency contraception pill plus antibiotics for STDs. She was also given anti-retroviral medication to prevent HIV infection and counseled that the medication was not a guarantee of prevention and she needed follow-up tests in six months. A counselor also talked with her and gave her a list of crisis counseling referrals for sexual assault victims.

The assailant, already in custody, was charged with sexual assault, and Lisa was listed as the complaining witness. A lady from the Victim Witness Division met with Lisa to explain the court process and help her fill out two forms. The first was a Victim Impact Statement, which would be used by the judge at sentencing to consider what physical and emotional impact the crime has had on her. The other was a Victim Information Sheet that would be used by the prosecutor to notify her if the defendant is released.

A few weeks later, Lisa received a notice which stated: "As a victim of sexual assault, once the defendant is indicted, you have the right under the Texas Criminal Procedure Code to request that the judge order the defendant to undergo a medical test for sexually-transmitted diseases (including AIDS)." Lisa exercised that right, and some time later, she received a letter stating that her assailant had tested negative for sexually-transmitted diseases, including HIV. That was a relief! *At least we don't have to worry about that anymore.*

Her assailant had also been wanted in a different county on another rape charge and is still serving time.

Chapter 11

"They destroyed my house!"

At about four o'clock in the morning a month or so later, the phone rang. It was Lisa, of course. Considering the hour, I knew it wasn't good news.

"Mom!" she wailed breathlessly. "I was visiting some friends in Montrose yesterday, and while I was out with them, someone took my car. I've been looking for it and calling all around all night. I don't know where it is and I want to come home. I've been walking around on the streets all night."

I refused to pick her up and told her to stay there and try to find her car. Around 6 a.m., she appeared at our front door with a taxicab and wanted me to pay for the cab, approximately $46. I instructed the cab driver take her to her townhome, and I paid him $50. She was beyond upset because she loved her car.

Three hours later, she called and said she had swallowed a bottle of pills (her prescription of Pexeva) because she was tired of living her horrible life. Despite being relatively certain that she was faking a suicide attempt, I called 911. When paramedics arrived on the scene, she refused their treatment and wouldn't let them into her townhome.

Five minutes later, Amber, one of Lisa's street friends who, along with her boyfriend Sam, had been staying with Lisa, called me to say that the Pexeva bottle was empty and she was calling 911 again and would make sure Lisa got treatment this time. Still convinced that Lisa had not taken the pills and was simply using drama to get attention, I went back to bed. *But I didn't sleep.*

When the ambulance arrived, Lisa locked herself in the townhome and refused to let them in. Amber called me again, frantic, asking me what she should do. I asked to speak to the EMT, who said they would have to break down the door if she didn't open it. The EMT suggested I come there to help defuse the situation.

When I arrived, in the parking lot in front of her townhome were an ambulance and four police cars with about six police officers milling around. Lisa was sitting up on a stretcher in the ambulance, wrapped in a blanket, being written a ticket by one of the policemen. Apparently, when she had finally opened the door to let the EMTs inside, they rushed inside before she could change her mind. In the confusion, she hit one of the EMTs in the face. He then called the police.

As soon as the ticket for assaulting the EMT was written, the ambulance took her to the emergency room, from where she was released later in the day. I knew she was no longer in any danger, so I did not go to the hospital. Consequently, I don't know what treatment she received or what was pumped out of her stomach. *If anything.*

I monitored her emotional state for the next two days by visiting several times, and I made sure she took her prescribed medications as instructed. During that time, she was relieved to receive a phone call from the owner of a downtown car repair shop telling her that someone had dumped a car in his lot. He had found Lisa's registration papers in the glove box and called her. She immediately asked a friend to drive her to the shop so she could retrieve her car. It was not damaged, but it was out of gas.

On the third day after the Pexeva incident, I did not hear from her at all. When she finally answered my phone calls the next morning, she sleepily admitted that she was at someone-named Manny's home.

"Who is taking care of your dogs, Lisa?"

"Sam and Amber are staying there and taking care of the dogs," she replied, still groggy from sleep.

"Why did you leave?" I pressed.

"Because I was tired of having Amber and Sam at my house and I had asked them to leave, but they wouldn't. So I left instead."

She leaves her own home because she couldn't make her visitors leave! This was backwards!

"Lisa!" I admonished. "When someone is staying with you and you no longer want them there, THEY are the ones who have to leave—not you."

"But, Mom," she whined, "they said they had no place to go, and they wouldn't leave."

"I want you to get into your car and drive back home right now. If you want them to leave and they refuse, tell them you are going to call the police. If you can't bring yourself to tell them, then I will."

Reluctantly, she agreed. About two hours later, she called, incoherently screaming into the phone, "They destroyed my house! They destroyed my house! Mom, come quick! They destroyed my house!"

I couldn't get there fast enough. When I pulled into the parking lot, Lisa was standing next to her car, screaming and pointing at the windshield, which had been bashed in.

"What happened?" I yelled as I leaped from my vehicle. While sobbing, she related the story.

"When I got home, I walked into the house and saw that it was a wreck. I guess Amber and Sam had gotten into a fight, and Sam took the sledgehammer from the closet and knocked holes in all the walls. They destroyed my sofa and threw an end table into the living room window. It was smashed and glass shattered everywhere. I ran out and was headed for my car to drive somewhere to call the police, and Sam ran after me. He swung the sledgehammer and smashed my windshield before I could get the car started, but I was able to drive away and get to the convenience store on the corner and call police. I waited there for the police to arrive, and they followed me to the house and told me to stay in my car while they went inside."

At this point I hurried to the front door of the townhome to see the damage for myself. It made me sick to my stomach. The entire place was a mess. It had been maliciously and criminally vandalized. You couldn't see the floor for the drywall chunks and dust that covered everything. There were huge holes in the walls, and nearly every piece of furniture in the living room was broken. The front window was now a million pieces. The vertical blinds were a tangled web on the floor. Even the front door had been torn from its hinges.

I took a deep breath, closed my eyes to escape the scene, and asked, "What did the police do?"

"I guess they talked to Amber and Sam, but I don't know what they told the police because the cops allowed them to leave. I watched them leave in a taxi, and they were carrying my television set. I ran to the policeman and told him that they were taking my television, and he told me that they had said it was theirs. By this time they were gone." *Some nerve to steal her television in plain sight, after destroying her home?*

"Didn't the police say ANYTHING?" I pressed.

"They gave me an incident report number and told me the homeowner *(me!)* would have to sort this out," Lisa replied.

Still sick to my stomach, I went through the house, taking photographs of the extensive damage. Upstairs I found the words "crack" and "whore" scribbled on the walls and more destruction. A bookcase was upended, and dozens of DVDs and music CDs were strewn about and had been stomped on.

Also upstairs, I found a friend of Lisa's, Stephanie, who had been hiding in the walk-in closet while the destruction was occurring because she was afraid of Amber and her boyfriend. Stephanie told me that when the police arrived, she had come out of hiding and confirmed to them that Amber and her boyfriend had done the damage.

I wrote up a statement with all the information that I thought could be helpful to the police, printed some photos of the damage, and drove to the nearby police command station.

The desk clerk refused to take the information and instructed me to call the "Burglary and Theft" division the following morning.

I tried all morning to get through to a B&T investigator and finally succeeded early in the afternoon. The investigator told me that I should have given the report to the desk clerk. So, I drove back to the command station and left the information with a clerk, a different one this time.

I notified the insurance company and called a restoration company (the type of people who come in and clean up after disasters like hurricanes and floods and other disasters). The townhome was definitely a disaster.

Chapter 12

Consequences

The restoration company arrived the next day. While they were working on the wreckage, we turned off the air conditioner because of the smashed windows and open doors. It was the middle of a hot, humid Texas summer, so the townhome was extremely hot inside.

To cool down, Lisa and Stephanie decided to ride around in Lisa's car, which was air conditioned. They stopped at the nearby convenience store and were approached by a young man in his mid-twenties who had just come out of the store. He asked if they would drive him to his apartment down the street. He said it was too hot to walk and would pay them five dollars.

They drove the young black man to his apartment at a complex about six blocks away. After dropping him off, they were stopped by police who, after determining that Lisa and Stephanie did not live in that complex, arrested both of them for criminal trespassing. We would later discover that it was an apartment complex the police had begun to monitor closely because of recent drug trafficking there. Many of the tenants were new and had relocated there from Louisiana and Mississippi after Hurricane Katrina.

Lisa called me from the city jail around 1 p.m., terrified and begging me to bail her out. I told her she would have to handle this problem herself because it was a mess she had gotten herself into. Personally, I felt that the criminal trespass charge was ridiculous. I was angrier that she had done something as stupid and dangerous as giving a ride to a stranger.

I advised her to ask for a public defender, but because she had a clean police record, she was released the next day on personal bond with instructions to appear in court on Tuesday and Friday of the next week.

Her car, an eight-year-old Toyota Corolla, was another matter. Having been towed by a police wrecker to an impound lot, we had to pay an impound fee of $288 to get it out. When Bill and I tried to start the engine, we discovered that the engine was locked up, ostensibly because it had been towed improperly.

Bill and I couldn't move it, so the car had to remain in the impound lot over the long Labor Day weekend, with an additional fee added every midnight.

We returned to the impound lot on Sept. 5 (day after Labor Day) but had to pay another $212 to the impound lot before they would release the car. Bill had arranged for the auto club to tow it twenty miles to my son's house so he could work on it. He knew a lot about cars and engines and was studying mechanical engineering at the University of Houston.

I didn't tell Lisa that her brother Brian was able to get the car running again, replaced several parts, and had cleaned it up, inside and out. I wanted her to think that her car was ruined as a result of her poor judgment.

I personally drove Lisa to her two scheduled court dates the following week, where a trial was set for a date in two weeks.

On the day of her trial, as I was on my way to pick her up, she called me and said I should turn around because she wasn't feeling well and had called the court and asked for a re-schedule. I doubted seriously if she was telling the truth, but I couldn't force her to go, so I turned around and went back home.

The next day, when I reminded her to call and re-schedule, she told me that the case had been settled for "time served" and it was all over. Again, I had my doubts, but decided to do nothing. I didn't know if I was deceiving myself into hoping what she said was true, or if I was simply resigned to letting her suffer the consequences if it wasn't.

Unfortunately, the following day I received a call from the court's pre-trial services, telling me that Lisa had told them she was in the hospital. Since she was not in the hospital and had lied, there was now a warrant out for her arrest.

The pre-trial services clerk told me that if Lisa came in voluntarily before 7:00 p.m. that same day, they would do everything they could to make sure her psychiatric disabilities were taken into consideration and the arrest would be much "nicer" than if the detectives had to go out and find her and arrest her.

I was furious with her for lying, but Bill and I remained calm and tried to make her understand that she was going to have to suffer consequences for her actions. It took awhile, but she finally acquiesced.

We walked into the jail at 6:45 p.m. with only fifteen minutes to spare. Lisa was taken into custody by a sheriff's deputy, and I was assured that the Mental Health-Mental Retardation Association (MH-MRA) would be called to take care of her psychiatric needs. MH-MRA provides mental health services—such as medication management—in the county jail system to offenders with mental impairments.

As she walked out the door in cuffs with the deputy, I clapped my hands over my ears and squeezed my eyes shut. It took a few minutes before I slowly lowered my hands and allowed my eyes to open. *That was my daughter that I had just allowed to be put in jail.*

We were doing the right thing, weren't we? After all, she needed to learn her lesson with natural consequences. She broke the law, so she must be punished. I wasn't sure. She wasn't like other children.

73

Chapter 13

County Jail

The next day I received about twenty collect calls from Lisa ($3.60 each, most of which I did not accept). She was crying hysterically and told me that it would be two weeks before she could be seen by MH-MRA (Mental Health-Mental Retardation Association) and that she was going crazy. I immediately called the Mental Health Association and left an urgent message for them to return my call.

After my classes, I drove to the Harris County Jail to visit her, and I experienced one of the most horrible and depressing experiences of my life. Visiting hours at the jail began at 4 p.m., so I checked in with the visitation officer. Inmates are only allowed one visitor per day, so the officer reviewed the log to verify that Lisa had not already received a visitor that day.

I was allowed to enter and was told to wait in a large, cold, uncomfortable room. Here I was checked for having "appropriate attire," that is, no revealing clothing such as tank tops, tube tops, or spaghetti strap dresses, no sleeves shorter than halfway down the upper arm, no skirt length above mid-thigh, and no gang-affiliated clothing. *I had no previous knowledge of these regulations, but thank goodness I passed the clothing inspection.* I also had to leave my purse and cell phone in a locker.

I looked around the room. There were about a dozen other people there, mostly women and children of all ages and appearance. I realized that despite the diversity, we all had something in common: We were all there to see someone in jail. However, it was clear that most of them had done this before. They were chatting normally, their children were laughing and jumping about, and they seemed to be free of the stress and anxiety that were gripping me in the gut.

My heartbeat was thudding in my ears when we were told at four o'clock that we could enter the elevator to go up to the visiting area. The experienced visitors knew where to go to get into a single-file line and pass through a highly-sensitive metal detector, so I followed.

The visiting area was small and extremely noisy because sound echoed off the tall cement walls and ceiling. Because it was so noisy, the inmates and their visitors had to shout at each other to be heard, further increasing the decibel level.

The visiting area was divided into two halves, partitioned by glass. Every three feet in the glass was an eight-inch, round, barred opening through which the inmates on one side could converse with family on the other side. There would not be any physical contact with one another.

As I waited my turn, a wave of depression, disbelief, and despair engulfed me. *What am I doing here? I'm a college professor, for goodness' sake. I've never been inside a jail. I've never even known anyone who had been in jail. Now I'm waiting to visit my daughter in jail. How did this happen? What do I tell her? That I'm sorry for putting her here? That it's her fault that she's here?*

I just stood there, dazed and overwhelmed by the sights and sounds of that room. I finally sat down, but I kept shifting uncomfortably in my chair as I waited for what seemed like hours.

After only about fifteen minutes, she was brought into the inmate side of the visiting area, looking disheveled and wearing the bright orange jumpsuit associated with jail inmates everywhere. My eyes studied her. Her face displayed genuine joy at seeing me but also underlying fear and fatigue.

There was no privacy, of course, so we couldn't have much of a conversation except for her telling me that she was scheduled to see the judge the next day and would ask for a public defender to represent her. She also said that she couldn't sleep with all the screaming and moaning by the other inmates and that she "would do anything to get out of this place."

Well, that's good, at least. Maybe, after this experience, she will think twice before doing something stupid. However, borderlines don't think like everyone else. What serves as a lesson for most people doesn't even register with borderlines.

I told her I loved her and to follow the advice of her lawyer and that everything would be okay.

The next morning, I received a return call from MH-MRA, confirming that since Lisa was not suicidal, she was not high on the list and would not be seen by the jail psychiatrist for about two weeks. The lady curtly added, "This is our process. We have over ten thousand inmates and only three doctors." I told her that Lisa had been diagnosed with bi-polar disorder, major depression, and borderline personality disorder and was taking medication for all three. I expressed my concern that going "cold turkey" off the meds for two weeks would put her in danger. I gave her the names of Lisa's three meds and the dosages, and she said she would do what she could.

The medication situation became moot when Lisa saw the judge in the afternoon. Upon the recommendation of her court-appointed attorney, she pled guilty to the criminal trespass charge. The judge dropped the charge of failure to appear in court, but accepted the guilty plea of criminal trespass and released her for "time served."

But she now had a criminal record. All because of her reckless decision to give a complete stranger a ride home for five dollars.

The repairs to the townhome continued, meanwhile, and were finally completed at a cost of $7,000, most of which was covered by insurance. During this same period, Lisa had to appear in court for assaulting the EMT in the Pexeva incident. An understanding judge dismissed the case because the complaining witness, the EMT, did not appear.

Chapter 14

Three Strikes and You're Out (of Cars)

Bill and I decided to let Lisa continue believing that her Corolla had been totally ruined by the poor tow job because we wanted to use its loss as a consequence that she could understand and apply directly to her actions. We anticipated that she would be begging for another car at some point, but we were wrong.

Instead, Lisa told us that having a car had caused all sorts of problems in her life, and she didn't want another one. She maintained that people "used" her just to take them places, and it just got her into trouble. That was fine with us. She lived near two different bus routes, which was one of the reasons we had bought the townhome in the first place.

The Toyota Corolla was not her first car. She had had three different vehicles within a span of three years. The first one was a six-year-old Hyundai Accent with 99,000 miles that we gave her for her twenty-first birthday after she successfully completed a driver training course and then passed the Texas Department of Public Safety knowledge and driving tests to earn her driver's license.

In less than a month, we had to put $700 worth of repairs on the car, and three months after that, we donated it to the Purple Heart charity because Lisa and Eric never checked the oil and had burned up the engine. Purple Heart arranged for free towing and gave us a nice tax deduction.

We gave her another chance because Bill was about to trade in his seven-year-old Mazda 626 for a new car. It had just under 100,000 miles and still ran fairly well, so he let Lisa have it. I don't know how or where she and Eric drove it, but soon it was in the shop with all sorts of transmission problems, broken mounts, brake issues, and you-name-it, costing over $1,500 to repair. With a couple of other brief shop visits, she managed to keep the Mazda running for another eighteen months before it, too, ended up with Purple Heart. *The irony wasn't lost on me. Those cars deserved a "Purple Heart" for all they went through with Lisa.*

The Toyota Corolla was her third and final chance. She had two strikes against her with the Hyundai and the Mazda, so we shopped long and hard for a reliable, older car. Research and conversations with many people convinced us that, despite its age of seven years and its high mileage of 147,000, a Corolla would last many more years and get excellent gas mileage. We found one at the very reasonable price of $3,500 and until Lisa's unfortunate criminal trespass incident, it served her well for nine months. Her brother fixed it up and drove it for another two years.

She hasn't owned a car since.

Chapter 15

Roll Over, Snow White

Lisa's intellectual and emotional limitations made finding a rewarding career for herself difficult. After the McDonald's experience, I knew that retail sales would never work.

I hoped that she could develop her love for animals into a career somehow, so I encouraged her to take two non-credit courses that related to animals at Houston Community College. One was called animal behavior management, in which she learned various types of reinforcement training and other training concepts as well as how to solve behavioral problems of wild, research, and domestic animals.

For her final exam she was required to purchase and train a white rat to do a trick. Lisa taught her rat, whom she named Snow White, to roll over on command. I was pretty impressed. Most of the other students were either not successful or had simply taught their rats to come when called (not too difficult if you are holding a treat). Lisa received the highest grade in the class.

At the end of the course, most of the students didn't want to keep their rats, so Lisa gladly accepted them and sold them to a local pet store. All except hers, that is.

Another HCC continuing education class she successfully completed was dog grooming. She learned basic grooming skills, including trimming nails and cleaning around eyes and ears, as well as the techniques to cut a variety of hair types and how to control the animals. For a short time, she even worked as an assistant to a professional dog groomer and gained valuable experience. Suddenly, however, that job ended, and Lisa wouldn't tell me why.

In one of her classes, Lisa met a lady who was a volunteer at the Houston Zoo. She encouraged Lisa to apply as an adult volunteer. After a background check, tuberculin skin test, and interview by the volunteer coordinator, Lisa was accepted into the program. As a new volunteer, she worked as a teacher's assistant to zoo educators, assisting with activity preparation, zoo tours, and the petting zoo.

I was so happy that she had found meaningful activity to raise her self-esteem and occupy her time. And she enjoyed it!

Soon there was a problem, however. When she first became a volunteer, she had a vehicle and was able to drive into downtown Houston to serve her volunteer hours. Six months later when she no longer had a car, it was difficult for her to get downtown because there was no direct bus line, so she stopped volunteering.

Chapter 16

The Contract

The letter we had sent to the townhome association had little effect on the number of violation notices we continued to receive. Now, however, most of them seemed to be legitimate and based on actual bylaw infractions. For example, "friends" from her street days continued to wander in and out or stay for days at a time. Furthermore, Lisa couldn't seem to get it into her head—*or didn't care enough*—that trash pickup was Mondays, Wednesdays, and Fridays and that on those days, trash could be put out between 6 a.m. and 9 a.m. only. The latest letter stated that Lisa had put out her trash Sunday evening.

We had already received several violation notices for this "when to put out trash" infraction over the previous two years, and each time I discussed it with Lisa and withheld the amount of the fine from her allowance. This time, however, the notice threatened to file a lawsuit against us and warned that we would be liable for all attorney fees and court costs, perhaps thousands of dollars.

The final straw of my patience was gone. Throughout her life, but especially after I became familiar with her borderline disorder, I had struggled with the core question of how much to help Lisa versus how much to let her flounder on her own. It was even difficult to know WHEN to intervene and when to pull back. There was no recipe, and there was no right answer because it was a moving target, depending on the situation. I felt "hooked" into her drama, stuck and trapped, and it was making me feel battered and exhausted, never on solid ground.

I decided that Lisa needed more structure—supportive structure. I had read that the inner worlds of borderlines are disorganized and chaotic, so an external world needs to be as predictable and consistent as possible. In that way she would know what to expect from me and what I expected from her.

To give Lisa this structure, I asked Bill to help me compose a contract with rules and expectations. I knew that putting things in writing gives people with mental illness a way to remember things that may seem simple or obvious to others, so we wrote it in the form of a letter.

"Dear Lisa,

This is your last chance. Here are the things you must do, or you will have to leave and will be back out on the streets. You and only you are renting this property from me. No one else can be there between 6:00 p.m. and 9:00 a.m.

You have ruined three cars. You will not get another one unless you get a job and earn the money yourself.

If you are ever convicted of a crime, you will leave the townhome. If you continue to violate townhome association rules, you will leave the townhome.

Your dog must be leashed the moment he steps outside your door, and you must carry a bag with you to pick up his poop EVERY time you walk her.

Your home and outside patio area must be kept clean. This means that no bags of trash may sit outside in the patio area, clothes must be washed and put away, floors must be swept and/or vacuumed, the bathroom and kitchen must be kept clean. I will come inside and inspect the house at least three times a week, unannounced. If it is not clean to my satisfaction, your allowance will be withheld until it is.

You may not call me between 10:00 p.m. and 8:00 a.m. Any threats of suicide between these hours will be ignored. There will be no more advances of money and no more cab fares paid.

Any damage to the property will be taken out of your future allowance payments.

Love, Mom and Bill"

I carefully went over each item individually with Lisa, making sure that she understood what was expected of her. I also explained to her that these rules didn't mean that we no longer loved her. They simply were reasonable boundaries for the good of all of us. Then we posted copies in several places throughout the townhome.

Lisa finally seemed to grasp the limits I had imposed. She continued to have some setbacks, but the frequency of violations dropped significantly. We only received an occasional letter saying she put the trash out too early, or the dog was off the leash, or excessive noise was coming from the unit.

Of course, it was very difficult for me to keep my end of the agreement, too. I relied heavily on Bill to support me when she called in the middle of the night, screaming that it was "an emergency." I also wished that we hadn't included that part about inspecting her house. I hated doing that, mostly because it was never very tidy. I usually ended up helping her clean up, which meant that I did most of the work. *But that's on me.*

Chapter 17

Jerry Springer?

Lisa became very skilled in the art of manipulation to get advances of what she called "her" money. Time and time again I fell for her manipulation, or as Bill aptly called it, lying. She lied consistently, about big things, small things, and even told lies when the truth would have worked to her better advantage. Sometimes she told a lie so often that it became the truth in her own mind. Manipulation and lying are prevalent in borderlines and often become habitual and uncontrollable.

Manipulation is one of many ways that people with BPD attempt to control others in their lives and influence their behavior. It is not usually a conscious decision on the part of the person with BPD to do this, but that doesn't mean that it's OK to allow it to continue.

Lisa's compulsive lies ranged from lying about feeling sick just to get out of doing something she didn't want to do— like clean her house—to lying about needing money for dog food or cleaning supplies when she really just wanted extra cash to buy cigarettes or marijuana. Other times there didn't seem to be any obvious reason for her lies, such as the time she told me a friend had died. She created an elaborate tale of how he had been gunned down in the streets as he walked to buy milk at the grocery store for his mother.

Another time she insisted that she needed money to fly to Chicago because she had been cast on the Jerry Springer Show. It didn't matter how many trick questions I asked about how and when and why she had been selected, she had a plausible, yet highly unlikely, answer ready.

If I didn't give her money, she erupted into an angry rage, cursing, yelling, screaming obscenities, and throwing things. Often she would threaten suicide or cut herself, and sometimes she would get so angry that she would punch holes in the walls of her home. She would telephone me over and over, dozens of times, trying to wear me down and make me responsible for her feelings. If I held my ground, I knew I was acting appropriately, but I was still consumed by guilt afterward.

Many times I yielded to her manipulation. I'm not proud of that fact, but giving her forty to sixty dollars seemed a small price to pay to avoid the emotional blow-ups, violent outbursts, and destructive behaviors that devastatingly tore at my very soul. It was also a small price to pay, it seemed, to have peace and serenity for a few days because whether or not she really used the money to go to Chicago, she knew she had to pretend that she did. As a result, there were no repeated phone calls or demands for a few days as she pretended to be away.

One example involved her volunteer work at the zoo. She had not worked there since her car had been towed during the criminal trespass case, but one afternoon shortly after the oil spill disaster in the Gulf of Mexico, she called me, all excited. She said that the Houston Zoo was sending some if its staff and volunteers to the New Orleans Zoo to help rescue pelicans and other wildlife in peril, and she wanted to go. She said she needed $150 to $200 for food, but that lodging and transportation would be provided.

Because of her history of lying and because this was a large sum of money, I told her that I would need confirmation from her supervisor that she indeed was going to be traveling to New Orleans with the volunteer crew. At this point, Lisa began screaming hysterically over the phone. She demanded to know why I was refusing her and insisted that her supervisor was unavailable and couldn't be reached. We went around and around.

"Lisa, just have Barbara (the volunteer supervisor) call me and confirm your story."

"But, Mom, I can't reach her,"

"Why not? You said she just called you to ask you to help, so she must be at a phone.

"She called me from a zoo phone, and she's not there anymore, and I don't know her cell number!"

"Well, call the zoo and get her cell number."

"They won't give it to me."

"Then you're just going to have to wait until she calls you back and ask her to call me."

"Noooooooooo, Mom! Why won't you let me do this?"

"I <u>will</u> let you do this, as soon as Barbara tells me your story checks out. You are asking for far too much money for me to just hand it over to you without corroboration."

More screams into the phone. "Mom, I <u>promise</u> to have her call you. How much money <u>can</u> you give me because I am going anyway, whether you give me money or not?"

"I'll give you forty dollars, no questions asked."

"Okay. I'll be there in ten minutes."

At this point, I knew she was lying because she so easily accepted a much smaller sum of money, but I gave her the money and didn't hear from her for over a day. I thought to myself, "Well, even if she was lying, forty dollars is a small price to pay for 24 hours of peace."

She finally called the next evening, saying she was in a motel and exhausted because she had been working all day, cleaning birds, but that she was really enjoying the experience and learning a lot. She had answers for all of my questions, such as "How many birds did you clean?" and "How many volunteers are helping?" and "What's the first thing you do when you start working on a bird?" However, I had not received a call from Barbara, nor had I received any photos of the rescue site taken from her cell phone, which I had asked for as proof.

The next time I heard from her was the next evening, when she called to say that she had slipped on some oil at the rescue center, had injured her back, and was on her way to the emergency room. A few hours later, she called to say that the zoo was flying her home because the ER doctor had said she needed bed rest.

She had craftily concocted an elaborate lie that brought her full circle, allowing her to "return home" credibly. *Or so she thought.* She maintains to this day that the story is true.

I feel as if there is a civil war going on inside of me, and both sides are losing.

Chapter 18

The Company You Keep
Will Determine the Trouble You Meet

One of the reasons Lisa always had people coming and going all day and all night was that she was terrified of being alone. It was also why she called me on the phone a dozen times a day. I learned that this intense fear of abandonment with an inability to be alone is a classic characteristic of borderlines. *That didn't make it any less aggravating to me.*

After Eric left the prior year, she had a steady string of roommates, or "squatters." In addition to causing problems with the townhome association, this desperation for companionship almost landed her in prison for ten years.

One evening as I was grading papers, the phone rang. It was a collect call from the Houston City Jail. My stomach tightened because I knew Lisa was in trouble again. She had been arrested as a result of an altercation at her townhome.

She was nearly incoherent as she wailed, "Mom, I didn't do anything! They arrested me for hitting Melinda, but I didn't do anything! It was the other girls who hit her! I don't know why they arrested me and I don't know why I'm here!"

One thing borderlines are good at is deflecting blame onto others to avoid personal responsibility, so I was skeptical about her innocence. However, I promised I would find out what I could, and I encouraged her to try to stay calm and not do anything dumb like hit anybody. It was all I could think of to say.

Bill and I didn't know what to do, so we went online to find out what to do when someone is arrested. We discovered that we should call a bail bond company, and they would investigate, contact the jail, and find information for us. I still had the business card of the bail bond company we had used for the taxi incident a few years earlier, so I called them. The agent who answered the phone was polite and professional. He assured me that he would let me know as soon as he had any information but that she probably had not even been booked and given an arrest number yet.

In the jail Lisa had access to a pay phone, and the collect calls were continual. I told her I would answer her call only if I had any information, but she kept trying, every few minutes. The constant ringing was shredding my nerves.

Finally, the bail agent called and said that Lisa was being charged with aggravated robbery, which was a very serious offense and meant that she would be transferred to the county jail to await a bail hearing that would occur sometime within the next forty-eight hours. The judge would determine, based on her criminal record and the seriousness of the offense, the amount of bail.

Lisa was lucky. Her bail hearing was held before she was transferred to the county jail, and bail was set at $35,000. Under the Texas Penal Code, aggravated robbery is a felony of the first degree and defined as "committing robbery and causing serious bodily injury to another; uses or exhibits a deadly weapon." According to the Internet, the penalties in Texas for first degree felonies ranged from five to 99 years, or life.

I was paralyzed by the thought. "Life in prison" kept playing in a vicious loop in my mind. I nearly gagged with fear.

Lisa was adamant that she hadn't done anything wrong, and I believed her. I don't know why I believed her because she certainly had lied to me countless times before about much less serious things. But, somehow I could feel authentic fear in her voice.

I drove downtown to the bail bond office to begin the bail process. I feared that dealing with the bail bond agents would be like dealing with a sordid business since they are constantly working with accused criminals, but it's simply a business like any other. The agents were all very busy, answering calls and helping clients. I was given a lengthy information form on which I had to provide financial information and at least ten personal references with addresses and phone numbers. The kind and efficient agent patiently described the process to me between his phone calls. He explained that the bail bond company pledges to pay the full amount of the bond if the defendant (Lisa) does not appear in court. For this surety, I would pay him ten per cent, or $3,500, and I signed an agreement to that effect.

Another important form that I had to sign guaranteed that Lisa would be present at all court-mandated appointments and follow the specific regulations outlined in the form. If a violation of the agreement in the bail bond forms occurred, I could possibly forfeit the entire sum of the bail, or $35,000. Lisa's stipulated regulation was that she had to check in, or call, the bail bondsman EVERY day until her case was disposed of, which could be as much as a year if it went to trial.

There were also conditions set by the judge when he granted bail. In addition to staying away from any of the witnesses or complainants of the case and not traveling more than 100 miles from Houston, Lisa had to report to the court every week for a urine sample and drug test. If any drugs or alcohol was found in her specimen, she would go back to jail. I could only hope that Lisa would be able to comply with these onerous conditions.

The bail bond agent swiped my credit card for $3,500 and told me that it would probably be three or four hours before Lisa was released because the forms had to be reviewed and filed by the court. He instructed me to bring Lisa to his office as soon as she was released.

By the time Lisa called me to say she had been released, it was morning. I hadn't gotten any sleep and had spent most of the night in a downtown bail bondsman's office. I called a substitute to teach my classes and drove to the city jail to pick Lisa up. We went directly to the bail bond office, where she filled out more forms and received instructions regarding her regulations.

The agents were still very busy, so while we waited, Lisa, who was overjoyed to be out of jail, narrated to me her account of what had happened.

"Melinda came by the house. Amber and Tamika were upstairs with me. Lonnie was downstairs and let her in. She came upstairs and started arguing with Amber. Amber can't stand Melinda, so she started calling Melinda names. Amber and Melinda have hated each other since we were all living on the streets.

"Anyway, Lonnie came upstairs and said that either Amber or Melinda needed to leave, so Melinda went downstairs to leave. Amber and Tamika followed her, and I guess Amber grabbed the empty blue Skyy Vodka bottle from on top of my refrigerator and hit Melinda over the head several times.

"While Amber was hitting Melinda, Tamika grabbed Melinda's purse and was going through it, looking for money, I guess. She didn't find any, so she pushed Melinda into the pantry door, yelling, "You don't have any money, bitch?" Then she grabbed the vodka bottle from Amber and hit Melinda in the face with it. There was blood everywhere running down her face and down her arms."

Horrified, I interrupted, "Where were you when all this was happening?"

"I was on the stairs looking down into the living room, and I was screaming and trying to get down the stairs to help Melinda, but Lonnie held me back and said, 'Stay out of it, Thumper!' Then Melinda stumbled out the door as Tamika was yelling, "Get out of here, bitch!"

The story she told begged my next question, "Why did Melinda have YOU arrested?"

"I don't know," Lisa replied. *Her usual answer for everything.* "But Lonnie will tell you that I didn't have anything to do with it."

"Where is Melinda now?"

"I think she's in the hospital, but she is going to be arrested, too, when she gets out because she has outstanding warrants."

What a mess.

Again, I was presented with the dilemma of whether or not to help her out or let her suffer the consequences. I checked out her story with her friend Lonnie, who was still at Lisa's townhome, and then called Bill. Together we decided that since this was a very serious charge that she did not seem to be guilty of, we needed to get legal counsel.

I had no idea whom to call. I asked one of the bond agents if she could help me find an attorney. She told me that legally she was not allowed to recommend anyone, but that there was a criminal defense attorney in the office next door that could give me information.

That was all I needed to hear. Lisa and I walked next door and made an appointment for two o'clock later that same day. We ate lunch at a nearby sandwich shop before arriving fifteen minutes early for our appointment with the attorney. At precisely two o'clock we were called in.

The attorney, Bob Williams, was middle-aged, charming, and a straight shooter. He immediately looked up Melinda's criminal record and found she had previously served time for theft on two occasions, once for twenty days and the other time for ten days. She had also served thirty days for possession and fifteen days for prostitution. Bob said it would be a piece of cake to impeach her credibility if the case went to trial. However, he felt strongly that the case would never reach the point of trial and that he could get it dismissed IF he could find Melissa and get her to recant her allegations. *That was a big IF.*

I swallowed hard and asked the salient questions, "Will you take the case and what will you charge?" He replied that his fee was ten thousand dollars, up front, cash or credit card. This fee would cover the entire case until its disposition, either by dismissal or by trial. In other words, if Bob got it dismissed next week or if he had to try the case in court a year from now, it was still ten thousand dollars. *To be paid now.*

Bill gave me the go-ahead to pay him, so Bob got going. Lisa began her irksome responsibilities of daily calls to the bail bondsman and weekly submission of urine samples. So far, somehow, her samples had been clean.

In a few days, we received a copy of the Probable Cause Affidavit signed by the police officer who spoke with Melinda in the hospital. Its grave wording stated Lisa and Amber "intentionally and knowingly committed the offense of aggravated robbery" against Melinda using a bottle as a "deadly weapon." The rest of the affidavit expressed what Lisa told me had happened—with one glaring difference. Instead of listing

Tamika as the person who had hit her, the affidavit named Lisa. There was no mention of Tamika.

Bob, meanwhile, had stayed on task chasing Melinda and had tracked her down. She was still at the hospital, having applied for and received a victim compensation package from the county. The purpose of the Texas Crime Victims' Compensation Program is to help eligible victims of crime with some of the expenses needed for medical bills. If one has no Medicaid or other type of insurance, the State will pay up to $25,000 for medical bills. So Melinda had remained in the hospital for awhile.

The fact that she was staying in the hospital a few days worked to our advantage because it was easier for Bob to track her down and get a more accurate statement from her than what she had given the police.

Bob and his charm were able to get from Melinda a statement in her own handwriting on a piece of notebook paper. She stated that it was Amber and Tamika, not Lisa, who hit her and robbed her of her purse and cell phone. She further stated that Lisa was a good person with a great heart who has helped her (Melinda) on many occasions, and who is innocent of the charge. She concluded by asking the district attorney's office to dismiss the robbery charge against Lisa and certified that the statement was made of her own free will and is true.

Bob's secretary typed up the handwritten statement, and an appointment was made with Melinda to come to Bob's office and sign it in the presence of a Notary Public. We had a few anxious moments when Melinda didn't show up as scheduled, but Bob was able to locate her and get her signature the following day.

Bob told me that in his conversation with Melinda, he found that she never really intended to get Lisa in trouble, but when Melinda talked to the police, she didn't know the other two girls' names. She knew Lisa's full name, but she knew Amber by her first name only and didn't know Tamika at all. When the police entered Lisa's full name into their computer database, the report of the incident when Amber and her boyfriend trashed Lisa's townhome came up. They assumed it was the same Amber with the same Lisa, so they filed the charges against the two of them.

The notarized statement and requests for dismissal of charges were filed, but it took another four weeks for the case to be officially dismissed. During that time, the daily calls to the bail bondsman and the weekly pee tests continued. I kept my fingers crossed that nothing would go wrong, and it didn't. After two months, $3,500 to the bail bondsman, and $10,000 to the attorney, Lisa was cleared of the charges.

You never think it's going to happen to you—being accused of a crime you didn't commit. It happens all the time, and often it happens to people who don't have the money to bond out of jail and hire a lawyer. These innocent people can end up behind bars for a long time.

Chapter 19

An Unexpected Mother's Day Gift

Lisa had allowed her Texas driver license to expire. Although she didn't have a car, she needed it for identification and, of course, if she wanted to drive someone else's car. The renewal process is usually easy and can be done online, but in her case she couldn't simply renew it because it had been expired for over a year. She had to re-apply in person as a new applicant and meet all the requirements, not to mention wait in a long line for hours on end.

While waiting for six hours in line, Lisa filled out the license application. One of the questions on the form required her to disclose if she had any psychiatric problems or had ever been hospitalized for a psychiatric illness. Lisa truthfully answered "yes."

When Lisa finally reached the clerk taking the applications, the clerk informed Lisa she could not proceed with the application process because she had a psychiatric history. She further advised Lisa to return to the driver's license office with information from her psychiatrist documenting her exact illness and medications and the effect they would have on her driving. Lisa was given a voucher so that she wouldn't have to wait in the long line the next time and could go directly to the front.

A week later, Lisa returned to the Texas Department of Public Safety, letter from psychiatrist in hand. A different clerk perused the document for a minute or two before informing Lisa that she couldn't determine the extent of Lisa's condition and was referring her to the State Medical Advisory Board for further evaluation.

The Medical Advisory Board is a panel of licensed doctors who review medical documentation relating to an individual's ability to drive. The board evaluates all medical information concerning an individual's medical condition and provides the Texas Department of Public Safety (DPS) with a recommendation on driver licensing.

Lisa never tells the truth. She had to choose this particular time to tell the truth?

We were still waiting to hear from the Medical Advisory Board when Lisa called me the Saturday morning before Mother's Day. She had spent the entire night before in the emergency room being treated for a stomach ailment, but she was home now and wanted to bring me flowers for Mother's Day.

Lisa had never done anything special for me or any other member of our family on holidays. She always expected to receive cards and gifts, but she never gave any. True to her borderline disorder, her concerns were always turned inward toward herself. Some therapists explain it as a constant attempt to fill a "black hole" inside themselves, so I never took it personally. As a result, I was shocked that she had flowers for me, and I must admit, pleased. *Could this be a sign that she is beginning to think about others?*

I asked, "How are you going to get here since you have no driver's license and no car?"

"Katy is going to take me," she said.

About a half hour later, I received a frantic call. "Mom, I've had an accident. Come quick!" she shrieked.

I rushed to where she was, about a half mile away, and found her sitting disconsolately on the curb next to a service station. Nearby in the parking lot sat her friend Katy's older-model car with a smashed front end. About ten feet away was a large Ford F-150, which looked to be fine except for a small dent in the front bumper.

Lisa jumped up and ran toward me when she saw me pulling in to the station. She immediately began explaining that

Katy had not wanted to get out of bed to drive her, so she let Lisa drive the car on the condition of putting some gas in it. As Lisa was leaving the gas station and attempting to pull out onto the street, she said her foot slipped off the brake and hit the gas pedal, accelerating into the street. The oncoming F-150 hit her front fender as it tried to stop. She attributed her actions to "still feeling groggy from all the medicine she had been given at the emergency room the night before."

Fortunately, no one was injured, but the driver of the F-150 had already called the police. I searched the glove box in Katy's car for proof of insurance but couldn't find any. Frantically, Lisa called Katy, who insisted that she had insurance but that her mother had the insurance papers.

I knew that this was looking worse and worse. Lisa had no driver's license and she had been driving a car with, I suspected, no insurance. My only consolation was that no one had been injured. I knew anything else could be taken care of, however inconvenient--or expensive.

A policeman arrived, and after assessing the situation, gave Lisa three tickets: one for failing to yield way, one for not having a valid driver's license, and another for driving a car with no insurance.

More court appearances.

Katy finally admitted she had no insurance and insisted we pay for repairs to her car, which was already a piece of junk with rusty dents in numerous places. After the accident the car was still drivable except that the front hood was dented to the point that it wouldn't close. One of Lisa's neighbors said that he could pound out the dent if he had a sledge hammer. I had an old sledge hammer that had belonged to my daddy, so I gave it to Lisa for her neighbor to use to fix the hood to the point it would close.

In the months after the accident, her driver's license was suspended by the State, and she has received numerous letters from a collection agency trying to collect $1,100 in damages to the other vehicle. *At least now we can stop battling the driver's license bureau about getting a license while on psychiatric medications. The State has taken care of it for us.*

She pleaded guilty in municipal court to all three charges, and I waited with trepidation to see how big her fine would be. I had already decided that if it were over $1,000, I would not pay it. She would have to do her time in jail instead.

The city attorney gave us a big break. He gave her the minimum fine of $240. Lisa and I both breathed huge sighs of relief. The last thing I wanted was for her to go to jail. Memories of her last incarceration still haunted me.

Chapter 20

Each Moment Is another Opportunity

A few weeks after Lisa's court appearance, I walked into a presentation at my church that changed my life. Still searching frantically for any insight into Lisa's affliction, Bill and I had read in our church bulletin that NAMI of West Houston would be giving a Mental Health Resources presentation at our church. NAMI is the National Alliance on Mental Illness, a non-profit, volunteer-driven organization that advocates for the millions of Americans affected by mental illness.

Depression, bi-polar disorder, and schizophrenia were discussed at length, and educational materials as well as information about support groups were disseminated. I was disappointed that nothing had been said about BPD, so after the session I approached the moderator. She apologized for not having any information about BPD but said she had a telephone number for a husband and wife who had just begun a support group for family members of BPD sufferers.

This telephone number led me to an invaluable support group, which then led to training and resources that helped not only me cope better but also my daughter cope better with her condition. It was a gift that would keep on giving.

I called the number to find out when and where the support group met. I didn't really know much about support groups or what they did, but I soon discovered that this one, which consisted of parents, spouses, friends, and children of borderlines, was a place that felt like home. The group met monthly at a church about twenty minutes from our home, and I immediately felt less isolated as I made connections with others facing similar challenges. There were family members of lawyers, of doctors, of high school dropouts, of children who had never held jobs and were still living at home, of spouses in prison, even a pastor's wife. Mental illness is an equal opportunity offender.

It was a place where we shared personal stories and expressed emotions in an atmosphere of acceptance, understanding, and encouragement. Speakers were sometimes brought in—from mental health professionals familiar with BPD to defense attorneys specializing in mental health issues—and resources were shared. I felt strengthened and empowered, and it was so helpful just getting to talk with other people who were in the same boat. Bill attended most of the meetings with me, and before long we were asked to be leaders of the group.

It was through the group that we heard about Family Connections, a research-based, twelve-week course for family members of borderlines. Modeled after NAMI's Family to Family course, the Family Connections course is coordinated by the National Alliance for Borderline Personality Disorder (NEA-BPD) to help BPD family members obtain the latest knowledge and research on BPD, receive support from others in similar situations, and develop skills for their own well-being. Bill and I became trained as Family Connections leaders during an intensive three-day session in Dallas.

Of the many valuable skills that the course teaches, it was the validation skill that turned out to be the most valuable to us, and it was also the one that I needed to practice the most. I learned that when my daughter was emotionally charged, I shouldn't respond with phrases like "Don't feel that way" and "Stop it." Those had never worked anyway to calm her down and had sometimes even escalated her, so I wanted to focus my energy on something that would work, which was to validate, or empathize with, her feelings. This didn't mean agreeing with her impulsive behaviors or her emotional rages, but instead acknowledging the legitimacy of her feelings. Instead of disagreeing with her feelings and telling her she shouldn't be feeling them (not an option for borderlines), I could try to say something like, "You must be so frustrated" or "I can see that you are hurting." *Validate the feeling without agreeing with the action. Validate. Empathize.*

The skill was so fresh on my mind that I was able to use it less than two hours after returning home from the Dallas training course for Family Connections leaders. Lisa called me in hysterics about some current crisis. I was tired from the trip, and the last thing I wanted was to deal with my child's emotional dysfunction, but I remembered what I had learned about validation. All I said was, "Lisa, I completely understand why you are upset. It would upset me, too."

There was silence on the other end for a moment or two. The next words I heard from her were calm and thoughtful. Her level of emotion had plummeted like a rock. Validation had worked! She had de-escalated simply because I was non-judgmental.

Healthy selfishness was another skill that wasn't going to come easy for me. Its premise was that we, as family members of a borderline, have a right to take care of ourselves first and be healthy. It's like the instructions we receive from flight attendants to place the oxygen mask on ourselves first and then help the child. If we develop our own anxieties, addictions, and depression from trying to help our borderline cope, we are no longer of any help to them. Our borderline family members cannot become our identities, and we must protect our own lives. *I guess I had already begun this when I let Lisa live on the streets when she turned eighteen.*

Chapter 21

Practicing Validation

My validation skills can be needed without notice and when least expected. I was between classes and in my office when my cell phone rang. Lisa was hysterical on the other end, and after several tries to understand her wails, she finally communicated that her best friend, 26-year-old Relle, had died in her sleep.

She and Lisa shared the same birth date, and she had lived with Lisa for over a year until the diabetes she had lived with all her life became so severe that Relle had to be hospitalized for weeks at a time. She could no longer work as a medical assistant, and she had all sorts of surgical procedures done, including an unsuccessful kidney transplant to replace her failed kidneys. Between hospitalizations, she lived with her sister and was transported by ambulance three times a week to the medical center for dialysis. This continued for about two years, but she never lost her sense of humor and zest for life. Losing her was devastating to Lisa.

I watched Lisa carefully during the next week because this was one of the toughest losses she had to face since the death of her granny. I stayed available by phone, and she called me at least ten times a day, as her fear of abandonment kicked in full force. She always gave some lame reason for calling: "My back hurts. I have a migraine. We need to get some flea medicine for the dogs. When can we go to Walmart?"

One evening about a week later, the call came.

"Mom, I'm having a hard time. I am really, really depressed."

"Oh, Sweetie, you have every right to be sad. You have just lost one of your best friends. Anyone would be very, very upset."

"But, Mom, I have a knife in my lap and I'm too sad to live. It's all so hopeless; I'm going to cut my wrist."

"Sweetie, I need for you to do me a favor."

"What?"

"I need for you to go into the kitchen and put the knife back into the drawer, okay?"

A minute of silence passes.

"Okay. It's back in the drawer."

"Now, let's talk about your sadness. Losing your friend must be so painful for you. I love you very much, and I want to help you deal with that pain. I think you have done a wonderful job of handling your feelings so far. You have come a long way since the days when you would lose control of yourself and become violent."

"Do you really think so?"

"Oh, absolutely. You called me BEFORE you cut yourself, didn't you? How many times in the past have you cut yourself and not tried to get help?"

"I just miss Relle so much. I feel so lonely now because I could always pick up the phone and call her, and she would have something funny to say."

"I know, Sweetie. I know. Let's think about the good times with her. Tell me about something funny that Relle did."

Laughs. "Well, one time when she was in the hospital and very loopy from the pain medication she was being given, she called me and said, 'I want to speak to Lady or Bubba.'" (Those were Lisa's dogs). "I asked her why she wanted to speak to them and not to me, and she said, 'Because I miss them. You come to visit me in the hospital, but they won't let Lady and Bubba visit, so I want to talk to them NOW.'"

Lisa laughed again and said, "Relle really loved my dogs."

"That's a cute story. We have a lot of wonderful memories, don't we?"

"Yes. She was an absolute angel and didn't have a mean bone in her body."

"Do you want to come and spend the night with us?"

"No, I think I'd rather stay at home. I'm beginning to feel calmer. I think I'll take my nighttime meds now and watch TV until I fall asleep."

"Okay, but call me if you need to talk, or if you can't sleep."

"I will. I love you."

"Love you, too."

I'll never know if she really had a knife in her lap. Borderlines often use threats to gain attention and manipulate, but the high rate of suicide attempts ad completions with this disorder make it a serious issue. I had to assume she did.

Chapter 22

Trick or Treat

It was Halloween afternoon, and Lisa had just turned twenty-eight. She was feeling lonely because her boyfriend had classes all day, so she asked me if she and I could go to Walmart to buy some food and supplies for her house.

We shopped in different parts of the giant store, and after about thirty minutes, we met at the checkout line. We were fourth in line, about normal for a weekend afternoon, when Lisa said she was going to the restroom. About five minutes later, all hell broke loose.

Just as I was about to unload our baskets onto the checkout conveyor, I looked up to find Lisa approaching me in tears, with four Walmart employees closely surrounding her.

She had a terrified look on her face as she tearfully whispered, "Mom, they caught me trying to steal some videos," before the employees whisked her away.

Stunned, I abandoned the two shopping baskets in the checkout line and followed as the store personnel led her into the security office. I tried to go in with her, but the store officials would not allow it because she was "of age," as they put it. They suggested that I continue about my shopping while they talk to her. Then they went inside, shut the door, and left me standing at the entrance, dazed and almost immobilized.

I managed to call Bill at home and informed him of what I knew. He suggested that I ask the store officials if they would release Lisa if I paid for the videos. I waited by the door until one of the employees came out about fifteen excruciating minutes later. I asked him to tell me what was going on. He related that Lisa had gone outside the store with four DVD videos in her purse, about $65 worth.

I asked him if I could pay for the videos and forget all of this. He explained that since the amount was greater than $50, store policy stated that they could not accept payment, and that they had already called the police. I mentioned that my daughter was emotionally disturbed in the hopes that they would have some mercy, but he tersely replied, "She already told us that."

I paced nervously outside the security office for another twenty minutes until Officer Dillon arrived and entered the security office. I recognized him as the same officer that had responded several times to Lisa's home because he had been trained in dealing with the emotionally disturbed. I was relieved to see him and knew that, being familiar with Lisa and her history, he would be compassionate and know how to handle her.

Call dispatchers are trained to identify mental disturbance calls and assign these calls to CIT trained officers. CIT, which stands for Crisis Intervention Team, trains officers to use de-escalation techniques if necessary when confronting a mentally ill individual. Otherwise, an untrained police officer could inadvertently approach in a manner which escalates the situation. On rare occasions, we have all heard media reports of mental health related calls that end in horrible tragedies, with officers or persons with mental illness being seriously or fatally wounded.

Another excruciating twenty minutes passed as I stood outside the closed door of the security office, watching shoppers hurrying into and out of the store. I felt a strange sense of not being there, of having been yanked inside out.

Then came the moment every mother has nightmares about. The security office door opened, and out came Officer Dillon with Lisa—in handcuffs. I winced and closed my eyes as if I had been struck.

Lisa was terrified and calling out, "Mom! Mom! They're taking me to jail!" I was still numb from the ordeal, so it was easy to remain calm. I asked Officer Dillon if I could accompany them to the police car and give her some medication. He allowed it, and I tried to assure her that everything would be all right.

He opened the back door to his police car, and she crawled into the seat, still in tears. They drove away, and I drove home to wait for information.

My numbness soon turned into acute pangs of devastation and betrayal. I wanted her to pay for what she had done and vowed to leave her in jail and not bail her out. Slowly, my anger plan transformed into *"well, maybe just overnight, just to teach her a lesson."*

Three hours later, I received a collect call from her at the city jail. Unfortunately, our new telephone service would not allow collect calls without a deposit of $50, so I had to make several attempts to put $50 into a phone account that was good for only ninety days and non-refundable. I shouldn't have worried about the non-refundable part because it took only four calls from the jail to use up the $50 deposit. I would eventually put in another $50 before the night was over.

Lisa's greatest fear was being transferred to the county jail, which would happen within a few hours if she was not bailed out. Her previous experience (and mine, when I visited her) struck horror into her, and her pleadings for me to get her out were desperate.

I contacted the same bondsman we had used for the aggravated robbery case. He said Lisa had been charged with a class B misdemeanor of theft in the amount of $50 to $500, and that bail was $1,000. The bond agent said they would "do it" for $150 plus filing charges of $15 and a runner's fee to deliver the bond of $35. We faxed paperwork back and forth for over an hour, and just as the runner was arriving at the city jail, Lisa called again, wailing that she had been transferred to the county jail.

I called the bond agent, who said that I would have to pay another $35 for the runner to now go to the county jail. The cost was up to $235.

Finally, an hour later (by now it was 10 p.m. on Halloween) the bond agent called to say that bail had been posted and that Lisa would be released in four to six hours. I decided to get some sleep because I knew that I would have to pick her up in the middle of the night, somewhere between 2 and 4 a.m.

I got little sleep, however, because Lisa called every hour or so. Calls from the holding area in the county jail were free, so she had no hesitation in calling every time she had a panicked urge. Each call detailed the filth and depravity of the county jail holding cell:

"It's like we are all cattle stuffed into this one big room. The sign says 'capacity 22' but I counted over 100, and they keep adding people. Mama, please get me out of here!

"People are shoulder to shoulder, and there is no place to sit down. We are packed in like sardines. Mama, please get me out of here!

"I've been in here for ten hours, and no one has been given anything to drink. The only fountain is right above the toilet, which is black with fungus and mold. Mama, please get me out of here!

"We finally each got a sandwich with a slice of bologna between two pieces of dry bread after ten hours. Mama, please get me out of here!

"The place is filthy. People have pissed in their pants, thrown up on themselves, and there are feces on the floor. Mama, please get me out of here!"

When, at six a.m., or eight hours after bail was supposedly posted, she was still incarcerated, I called the bond agent to find out what was taking so long. He said he'd get back to me. He didn't, so an hour later, I called him again. He said that a typographical error had been made on the paperwork and he would have to re-issue it and take it over to the jail again.

Another six hours passed before my daughter was ultimately released. She had spent nineteen hours as a guest of the City of Houston and County of Harris. I arranged for a substitute to teach my classes at HCC so that I could pick her up at the jail and accompany her to the bond company, where more paperwork was signed and her court date was determined.

Lisa apologized over and over to me for being so stupid and stealing. She said that she just had an impulse and couldn't stop herself. *Typical borderline trait.* She said that the jail was the closest thing to hell that she could imagine and never wanted to go back.

Of course, this was far from over. I decided to hire a criminal defense attorney to represent Lisa. A conviction for theft would follow her for the rest of her life and preclude her from ever finding a decent job. No employers want to hire someone who will steal from them. So far, all she had on her record was criminal trespassing, and I felt that most employers would be willing to overlook it as being in the wrong place at the wrong time. Moreover, the penalty for a class B misdemeanor in Texas is up to six months in jail and a $2,000 fine.

I didn't want to pay a criminal defense attorney $10,000 up front as I did with the aggravated assault charge three years earlier, so I told Lisa it was going to be her responsibility to look over the dozens of letters she had received from attorneys soliciting her as a client during the weeks after her arrest and booking. Most of them began with similar statements: "Your arrest is just the beginning of the potentially long and difficult process that was started by the arrest." *I was beginning to understand that very well.*

We needed somebody who was reputable and experienced in criminal defense, but there was none that stood out from the others. Lisa chose one based on the lowest advertised fee and set up an appointment. *Unfortunately, in most cases the advertised price is never the one you end up actually paying.*

The criminal defense attorney, Mr. Malek, was sincere in his approach and determined to get the case against Lisa dismissed. His strategy was to base his defense on Lisa's mental disorders, thus arguing that she was unable to recognize the consequences of her actions.

Unfortunately, the district attorney was not easy to convince. There was a total of four preliminary hearings, and at each one, the prosecutor asked for more evidence. In addition, there were court expenses of $400 that I had to pay each of the three times the case was reset.

We provided the district attorney's office documentation of Lisa's illness, scientific research on borderline personality disorder, and a letter from her psychiatrist listing her medications and attesting that Lisa was undergoing weekly psychotherapy. In the meantime, there were the mandatory weekly phone calls to the bail bonding company and the periodic urine samples for the court.

Finally, after five months and four pre-trial hearings, the district attorney agreed to drop the charges.

Chapter 23

Where Is My Starbucks Card?

The clear and present threat of jail may have worked to deter Lisa from stealing from stores, but it didn't keep her from stealing from me. She was as adept as a seasoned pickpocket. I couldn't understand how she did it, or even when, but on several occasions I opened my purse to pay for something and found it empty of cash. Once, when she was in a sharing, truthful mood, she admitted to taking cash from my wallet in my purse, which was on the floorboard of the front seat, on several occasions right in front of my eyes while I was driving. After that confession I placed my purse on the back seat when she was in the front seat with me.

Even that did not deter her. One day, she and I were grocery shopping and I had been trying to teach her how to select healthful, yet modestly-priced food items. As we pulled out of the parking lot, I double-checked where my purse was. It wasn't on the back seat where I had placed it. I asked Lisa to check the floor to see if it had fallen. She replied that it was indeed on the back floorboard and would return it to the seat.

That process took just a second too long, which triggered my suspicion. I stopped the car and looked into my purse. All of my cash was gone. I made her open her purse, and there, loosely shoved into a side pocket, were the tens, fives, and ones from my purse.

I tried to use my Family Connections training to emotionally separate myself from the situation, but I couldn't help myself and in a hurt and angry voice asked, "How could you do this, Lisa, after all the food I just bought for you?"

There was complete silence the rest of the way to her townhome. She unloaded her grocery bags and walked into her house. I drove away and used the time to calm myself. Halfway home, I received a text: "I didn't steal anything, but you think I did, so by the time you read this I will be dead."

Of the many parental decisions I have had to make, reacting to suicide threats is the most gut wrenching. Over the years, she made dozens of suicide threats, and all of them sent me into a panic. Although nearly all borderlines try at some point to escape their intense emotional pain with suicide attempts, most attempts are never fulfilled. However, ten per cent of those who attempt suicide complete it, whether by determination or by accident, for example, when help does not arrive as soon as they anticipated. It was this ten per cent I always worried about. Something could go wrong: she might not reach me, or I might not arrive in time, or she would get too drowsy from an overdose to call 911, or the slash on her wrists would be too deep.

However, I had gotten better at assessing risk and distinguishing true despair and suicidality from manipulation and blame deflection. Don't get me wrong; they are all coping mechanisms for her, and I take them all seriously, but I had learned the small signs differentiating between a life-threatening event and an attention-seeking gesture. This one seemed to be a clear attempt at deflecting blame from herself, making ME somehow responsible for her stealing attempt, so I neither panicked nor responded. She was probably afraid that she had really alienated me and was trying to find out how angry I was.

I didn't trust my instincts one-hundred percent, however, so a few minutes later I called her. I didn't want her to know I was trying to verify that she was all right, so in a normal voice I simply reminded her to refrigerate the chicken we had bought. My little ruse enabled me to check on her and show her that I was still there for her.

Later in the day she called, and, with both of us having had an opportunity to think about the episode, we talked about it. I calmly reminded her that stealing was wrong and that she had lost some of my trust and would have to re-earn it.

Her stealing, as we had come to understand, was a result of poor impulse control. People with BPD live under the power of their impulses. Most people can usually override out-of-control impulses, but for borderlines, emotions are in the driver's seat steering their thinking. Attempts at self-restraint usually fail. Rather than dealing with her negative thoughts and emotions, Lisa would impulsively grab a quick fix to feel temporary relief, to feel alive.

Two weeks later, I pulled into a Starbucks drive-through and tried to pay with my Starbucks gift card. Not only was my Starbucks card missing, but the zippered pouch I kept it in was also gone.

Because of the times I had tried to pay for something and discovered my purse to be empty, I had stashed a small pouch in the car with emergency money (about $40 in cash), my Starbucks gift card (worth about $40), and a handful of quarters for the compressed air machine when I needed to put air in my tires. I thought it was in a hiding place that Lisa couldn't find.

I didn't know how long the emergency pouch had been missing, but I immediately knew Lisa was the culprit. What confused me, however, was the question of when she would have had the time to search the car for it. Then it hit me. A few days earlier, I needed to get some money out of an ATM, and Lisa was with me in the car. I didn't want to go to the drive-through ATM because I didn't want Lisa to see me punch in my pin number, so I left her in the car for about three minutes as I used the walk-up machine. That's when she must have opened every compartment in the car to find the pouch.

I was angry and should have waited to call her. *Stealing money was one thing, but stealing my Starbucks card was the final straw.* I called her immediately and told her that I knew she had taken the bag. She vehemently denied it, but I knew in my heart that she had stolen it. She maintained her denial, knowing that I had no proof that she had done it. *I can't let her into my house because she steals. Now I can't let her into my car either?*

About six months later, as I was helping clean her pigsty of a townhome, I found the pouch, empty, in one of her kitchen drawers.

Chapter 24

"In therapy I see myself in
the mirror differently."

*– Ricky Williams, Texas Longhorns'
Heisman Trophy winner*

With the help of the validation techniques I had learned with the Family Connections course, I began to react more calmly to Lisa's borderline episodes. If I remained calm, often so did she. However, her biggest breakthrough came when we found the right therapist.

Finding a therapist was frustrating and emotionally trying for both Lisa and me. For one reason, there is a limited number of providers on Medicaid's approved list. Some of them refused to take a borderline patient because borderlines are perhaps the most challenging types of patients to treat and can be emotionally draining for the therapist with their frequent phone calls, agitation, and frequent threats of suicide. The extra patience and time required to treat borderlines, in today's political climate, often are not adequately recognized or reimbursed by insurance companies.

Most of the remaining therapists on the list didn't understand the disorder and had no idea how to treat borderlines. They used techniques that either didn't work or that Lisa wouldn't cooperate with, and she didn't trust any of them.

Lisa went through a half dozen therapists before we found Carol. Carol was a Godsend because unlike all of the other therapists, she actually liked borderlines. Through active engagement, she was able to guide Lisa through her highly changeable moods, her intense anger, and her impulsiveness. She was empathetic and accepted Lisa for who she was, while simultaneously promoting change. Lisa felt a sense of connection, and they built a strong bond with each other.

Lisa's therapist utilized two types of therapy, cognitive behavioral therapy (CBT) and dialectical behavior therapy (DBT). CBT is a type of psychotherapy that targets how the borderline thinks and behaves about situations and is very focused on the present, which means little talking is done about the past. DBT is a derivative of CBT and is considered the leading therapy for borderline personality disorder. Devised by Dr. Marsha Linehan, DBT helps patients identify the type of thoughts that makes their lives challenging and then learn different ways to think and react. It teaches how to feel intense emotions and see them through.

BPDs have dangerous ways, such as drugs and self-harm, to calm themselves down when they get emotionally upset. Carol taught Lisa self-soothing techniques like listening to music, looking at photographs or scrapbooking, taking a walk or a bath, playing with her dog, or going for a swim. When Lisa engaged in these strategies with a determined focus, her mood would almost always improve.

In order to obtain the best results from her therapy, however, it was crucial for Lisa to manage her other mental and physical health conditions as well. Almost 100% of borderlines have comorbid diagnoses, which means two or more co-existing conditions. Lisa certainly had a long list of diagnoses, so it was crucial to continue balancing her neurochemistry by taking her medication as prescribed by her psychiatrist: the antipsychotic Haldol for schizophrenic symptoms (hearing voices in her head), Seroquel for depression, Cogentin for reversing the side effects of the antipsychotic, Xanax for anxiety and panic attacks, Lamictal for mood disorder, and Ambien for sleep.

Managing her meds was extremely difficult for Lisa. Some borderlines refuse to take their prescribed drugs because they deny having an illness. That wasn't Lisa. She readily accepted her condition because she was relieved that there was an acceptable diagnosis for the craziness she felt. Lisa often didn't take her meds for three other reasons. First, she often forgot. This was most likely a side effect of her powerful medications, which made her confused.

Second, she didn't like the way the meds made her feel. Indeed, her prescription drugs carried a laundry list of side effects from drowsiness, grogginess, and lack of coordination to migraines and dry mouth, all of which she experienced. The third reason was money. With her connections to the street culture, she could sell her pills for a lot of money. One Xanax or one Seroquel tablet could bring her five to ten dollars on the street.

When she didn't take her medication, an entirely new "can of worms" opened. Not only were her psychological symptoms no longer managed, but she often experienced withdrawal with nausea, anxiety, restlessness, disorientation, insomnia, and headaches.

For awhile I called in her medication renewals myself and then picked up her meds from the pharmacy. Before I gave them to her, I kept back some pills for withdrawal emergencies. Finally, I got tired of enabling her inability (or lack of desire) to think ahead, so I let her manage her own medication. It was difficult for me to allow her to experience the consequences of withdrawal, but I hoped the terrible withdrawal symptoms would teach her a lesson.

It didn't, and she still sold her pills when she wanted money, thus having to suffer the repercussions of withdrawal, suicidal ideations, and hallucinations when she ran out before the pharmacy would refill them. Unlike most people, she couldn't seem to learn from her mistakes.

After many months of wrangling with this problem, we finally compromised on a solution. I bought a pill box with compartments for each day of the week, and I began dispensing one week's medication at a time. Soon, however, even a week's worth of medication was too much for her to cope with. She would call, wailing that she had lost them, that someone had stolen them, or my favorite: They fell in a mud puddle and disintegrated. I knew she had probably sold them.

I began doling out only two days of medication at a time, and this worked much better. It seems that she is less tempted to sell her pills if she has only two. *Whatever works.*

Why did I even bother? Why not just let her suffer the consequences? I probably should have, but I was taking the easy way out. It was easier to monitor her medications myself than deal with the consequences of being off her meds, like suicide attempts, for example.

Chapter 25

Meeting the Crack Dealer

Lisa had a new live-in boyfriend, her first since Eric moved out. John didn't have a job or a place to live, so whether he truly cared for her or not, shacking up with Lisa was a good thing with free room and board that we provided. It actually was a win-win situation for us, too, because he kept the would-be squatters out of the house. We no longer received violation letters from the townhome association for "too many people staying at the unit."

Another perk was that John guarded and dispensed Lisa's medication. He kept it in a locked box and made sure she took it as prescribed. Unfortunately, if she took her meds as prescribed, she did a lot of sleeping. John complained she was always asleep, and finally, after about six months, he left, too. *Abandoned again—here we go. I waited for another suicide attempt.*

It didn't take long for the call to come in. She had sold her television set to buy enough crack to kill herself, she said.

Here we go again. When I arrived at her place, Lisa was already suffering the "crash" stage—exhausted, depressed, and agitated. She admitted that she had smoked the crack several hours ago and thus was past the critical overdose period. However, she must have bought a lot of crack because she still owed the dealer $50 in addition to the television she had already given him. She begged me to give her the money or he would "beat me up or kill me," she sobbed, "because he lives in this townhome complex."

What should I do? I can't give her the money because she may go out and buy more drugs with it. Will I be enabling her if I bail her out of the jam? Probably. But I've got to do it. I want this guy out of her life. Is she telling the truth about this dealer being dangerous?

I decided to pay off her debt to the drug dealer, but I refused to give her the money to do it. I thought she might use it to buy more drugs. I told her I would give it to the dealer myself. *Oh, my gosh, what was I thinking?*

Lisa resisted, but I insisted, so she called the guy and said we would meet him in the parking lot of the townhome complex. I made Lisa stay inside and watch for him from her upstairs bedroom window while I waited in my car in the parking lot. Always thinking ahead, I wanted her observing from inside in case something went wrong and police had to be called. *Right...if I were really thinking, I wouldn't be doing this.*

I didn't know what to expect. Would he be on foot? Would he be armed? Would he be drugged out? Pictures of all the drug dealers I had seen on TV raced through my mind like a video on fast-forward. Pretty soon my cell phone rang.

"Mom, he's coming through the entrance gate. He's in a silver Cadillac Escalade."

Cadillac Escalade? That's a $75,000 vehicle! I guess the illegal drug business is pretty profitable.

He pulled up next to me in my twelve-year-old Chevrolet Blazer and stayed inside his vehicle, engine running. He rolled down the passenger window, which was next to my driver side window, which I rolled down. He was dressed in stylish clothes and had a diamond earring in his ear.

I spoke first. "I understand Lisa owes you money."

He nodded, but he didn't say anything.

"Is it $50?"

Another nod.

I opened my car door and reached into his open window with the $50 in my hand. He took it without saying a word.

My mind was screaming, "Tell him to stay away from your daughter. Tell him that if he ever sells her drugs again, you will call the cops because you have his license plate number. Tell him…"

But I was too scared. I just wanted him to take the $50 and leave. Which he did.

I realized I was trembling as I took down his plate number and got out of the car. On legs that felt like rubber, I walked to the end of the street to see where he would park his Escalade and which townhome he would enter. *I don't know why. Did I think I was going to turn him into the cops? Then what? There was no evidence, and if he found out, Lisa or I could be in danger. Too many cop shows on TV.*

On my way home, I called Carol and related what happened. I was so upset that Lisa had turned to drugs and was afraid she was going to become dependent on them. Borderlines are at unusually high risk of drug or alcohol abuse because of their emotional instability and impulsive behavior. They use drugs to self-medicate their pain of abandonment fears and other emotional issues they cannot deal with.

"Do I need to put her into rehab?" I asked Carol.

"No, this is just one of her borderline episodes. Bring her in tomorrow, and she and I will talk."

When I arrived home, my husband put his arm around me, and I buried my face in his shoulder and sobbed. I thank God I have a husband as understanding and supportive as Bill.

Instead of being angry that I had been out the entire afternoon with Lisa instead of at home with him, he had rushed to greet me, saying "I am so sorry you have had to deal with this all afternoon." He didn't know yet exactly what I had been dealing with, however.

After we collapsed on the sofa and I told him the story, he was not too happy with me for meeting with the drug dealer. Neither was my son, Brian. They both made me promise never to do it again.

Chapter 26

"I didn't punch anyone or break down in tears.

Some days the small victories

are all you achieve." *—Molly Ringle*

Although Lisa's quality of life improved greatly after she began seeing her therapist weekly, it was still no bowl of cherries. She continued making impulsive, bad decisions.

On one occasion, she became irate when I wouldn't give her any money, so she punched her hand into the well-supported wooden gate to her patio. The howl of pain made her temporarily forget her anger as she held her hand gingerly and mournfully announced that she thought it was broken.

"You made me break my hand," she screamed, the anger returning.

"I made you break it?" I asked, incredulously. *I wasn't going to let her get by with that one.* "Your impulsive anger and dangerous acting out made you break your hand, not me." I took a breath and remembered that this explosive rage derived from her distorted borderline perception that I didn't care about her and that I wasn't meeting her perceived needs.

Later that day she found a way to the emergency room to have it x-rayed. The films showed she had indeed broken several bones in her hand.

On another occasion, she called the pharmacy to find out if her medications had been refilled. *I was the one who usually did this because I didn't trust her with full bottles of powerful psychiatric drugs.* This time, however, she beat me to it and decided to pick up her newly-refilled prescription without telling me. Anticipating that she was planning to sell them, her new boyfriend, Colt, confiscated the pill bottles and told her he had hidden them.

As soon as Colt fell asleep that evening around 11 p.m., Lisa began searching the townhome for the pills. One of the first places where she tried to look was the attic. As she was trying to remove the large, heavy cover to the attic's opening, it fell on her foot. She called me, wailing, "Moooom! Please pick up the phone! I know it's after ten o'clock, but I'm hurt!"

Already almost asleep, I picked up the phone and she related what had happened. "I need you to take me to the emergency room right now!" she demanded.

I was so angry with her for deceiving me about the prescription that I replied, "You can wait until morning. I'll take you then to see if anything is broken in your foot."

"Nooooooo," she wailed. "I need to go now. It's bleeding."

"Put ice on it, wrap it in a bandage, elevate it, and take two ibuprofen. Or you can wake Colt up and ask him to take you," I sleepily replied and hung up. *There. I've given her my advice. She's 29 years old, and it's time she took responsibility, BPD or no BPD.*

She proceeded to call me thirty-nine more times that night between 11 p.m. and 5 a.m. I counted them. Sometimes she screamed a message into the answering machine instructing me to pick up the phone, and other times she just hung up after a few rings. I didn't pick up any of the calls, but that didn't mean I got any sleep. I lay awake, wrought with guilt and anger, listening to the phone ring incessantly.

Around eight the following morning, the phone rang again, with a message from Lisa stating that she had gone to the emergency room (*I don't know how she got there*) and was given eight stitches in her big toe.

Her stealing impulses were still getting the best of her, too. A few weeks later, I was celebrating my sixtieth birthday with family and close friends at a local restaurant. Lisa was seated at a table with Bill and me, her brother, his wife, and his baby son.

Suddenly, Lisa was nowhere to be found. Immediately, I checked my purse, and as I expected, all of my money—about $40—was gone. It was difficult to have a good time the remainder of the evening, as I struggled with concern for her safety, anger at her for stealing, and a throbbing disappointment that she would do this on my big day.

Some months later, about two months before her thirtieth birthday. I was getting ready to go to a dinner party with my husband when the phone rang.

"Mom, I just wanted to say I love you and that I'll see you on the other side."

"What are you talking about? What have you done?" I demanded, taken totally by surprise. My stomach felt as if it had been hit by a hand grenade because I knew that "I'll see you on the other side" was a euphemism for "I'm going to kill myself, and I'll see you in the afterlife."

"I just don't want to live anymore, so I swallowed all the pills in the house."

I gasped. "What did you take? How many did you take?"

"I haven't been taking my morning meds, so I gathered up all the pills and took them."

Although she had threatened suicide dozens of times previously, I took each one seriously. I knew each one was a cry for help and that borderlines were at greatest risk for suicide of any other group. Their emotions are so intensely painful—especially when they feel abandoned—that they genuinely think there is no way out.

Nonetheless, given Lisa's propensity for manipulation, I suddenly demanded, "Lisa, tell me the truth right now. Did you really take the pills, or is this an attempt to get Colt to pay attention to you?" *As if this request would make her tell the truth.* She had been complaining recently that her boyfriend, Colt, was acting distant and she was afraid he was planning to leave her. *Constant abandonment fears.*

"I really took them," she responded slowly and convincingly.

"I'm calling an ambulance."

"No, Mom, don't call an ambulance. Don't call an ambulance," she repeated.

"Why not?"

"Just don't." *Did her refusal to call an ambulance mean she was faking, or did it mean she really wanted to die and didn't want to be rescued? If she didn't want to be rescued, then why did she call me?*

"Where is Colt?" I wanted to know.

"He's upstairs playing a video game and doesn't know I took the pills. He..."

"Let me talk with Colt," I interrupted.

After several minutes Colt came on the line and seemed to be perplexed about what was going on. He said he had been busy upstairs and didn't know what Lisa had been doing downstairs.

"I want you to take her to the emergency room right now," I commanded.

Somewhat impatiently because I had interrupted his video game, he replied, "They'll just take her to the mental hospital if I do."

In disbelief I asked, "Would you rather she die from an overdose?"

He clearly didn't believe that she had taken the pills or didn't care because he handed the phone back to Lisa.

Family Connections skills were failing me right now. The thought of suicide activates my primitive reptilian brain, which overrides my rational thinking.

"Mom, it's okay. I just threw up all the pills. I hadn't taken enough to hurt me anyway."

I took a deep breath and stood quietly for a minute, collecting my thoughts. Rational thinking was returning, and I asked her if she realized that this was all a response to the psychological stress from her fear that Colt was going to leave her.

She meekly replied, "I guess so, but I've been so mean to him that I wouldn't blame him if he left."

"We talked a few minutes more about her feelings, and I encouraged her to talk with Colt about them. *If she could pry him away from his video game.* I told her I would call her back in about twenty minutes.

When I called back, I asked, "How is everything going?"

In a giggly voice she told me everything was fine and that they were hugging each other at that moment.

"Good. Hugs are good," was all I could say.

Then we went to our dinner party, where I had a huge glass of wine as soon as I arrived.

Chapter 27

Remember the Alamo

Lisa's thirtieth birthday brought another opportunity for Lisa to demonstrate her inability to control impulses and her inability to plan ahead. She loves visiting San Antonio, so as a birthday gift, Bill and I arranged a weekend there for her and Colt. She and I carefully planned a budget for the two days, itemizing food, entertainment, travel expenses, and hotel costs. She seemed to understand that if she followed the budget, she would have enough money for everything she wanted to do.

On Friday evening she called from San Antonio's River Walk to let me know they had arrived safely. The next day, I didn't discover that my cell phone battery was dead until two o'clock in the afternoon, so I blissfully didn't hear from her until 2:30, when I received a frantic call. I could immediately tell that she had not taken her morning meds and was having a borderline episode. She was practically screaming into the phone with one sentence rapidly followed the other.

"Mom, you didn't give me enough money. The hotel charged me more than you said it would, and you didn't give me enough money to cover the tax (*not true!*). Now I only have $100 left and I need it to buy gasoline to get home and that doesn't leave me anything to spend at Fiesta Texas. I don't know what to do! I'm just going to come back home. My birthday sucks."

When I could get a word in edgewise, I tried to use a calm voice to validate her anxiety and settle her down, but she refused to hear what I was saying.

"Lisa, it's 2:30 in the afternoon. The day is half over. Why aren't you already at Fiesta Texas?"

"Because I have been trying to call you. I'm freaking out! I don't know what to do!" she screamed.

"Have you taken your morning medications?"

"No," she replied.

"Lisa, you need to take them this very minute. I am going to hang up, and you can call me after you have taken your pills." I hung up.

Two minutes later, the phone rang again, but she was still nearly incoherent with uncontrolled emotion. I explained to her that she didn't need the entire $100 for gasoline and should put aside $60 for gasoline to get home, which left her $40 to spend for incidentals at Fiesta Texas. Her motel room and her park entrance ticket were already paid for, so she shouldn't need any more money for anything else.

"No!" she screamed. "That's not enough! I'm not going to Fiesta Texas with just $40! I need to rent a locker for my clothes at the Water Park, and water costs $9 a bottle, and $40 is just not enough! I need you to wire me some money. Now!" Then she repeated her frustration about this being "the worst birthday ever."

That remark hurt. *I had tried really hard to give her something that would make her happy for her thirtieth birthday.* Of course, I knew that she was having a borderline episode, but that didn't really make the words sting any less.

I calmly told her, "Lisa, I have told you what you need to do. Right now I can't talk to you anymore because my feelings are hurt." I hung up.

The next time I spoke with her was about twenty minutes later. The medications had kicked in, and she had spoken with her dad, who was wiring her some money and calling it a birthday present. She was much calmer and very apologetic, and her mood was a complete 180 degrees from what it had been twenty minutes earlier.

The sudden mood turnaround was also typical of borderlines and in this case probably resulted from a "perfect storm" of three factors: the pills had kicked in, she now had money from her dad, and her dad had "come through" in her time of need. She had been feeling rejected because her dad had not sent her a gift for her birthday. Perceived rejection is a trigger for borderlines.

She apologized profusely to me and couldn't stop talking about how wonderful her dad was for coming through with money to help her. She finally admitted why she was short of money. She and Colt had spent four times her budgeted amount on dinner and alcoholic beverages at a very expensive restaurant the night before.

I was furious with her dad for bailing her out, even if it was her birthday. I wanted her to feel the natural consequences of her actions and learn about reality. Her impulsive spending had resulted in no negative repercussions and indeed was actually rewarded by her dad. This was no way to get her to understand how the real world works. *I was also seething because he was now the hero for sending her $50 when I had spent five times that much on her.*

Chapter 28

The Physical Part of Mental Illness

Although borderline personality disorder is a dysfunction of the brain, the physical body also gets hammered. People with BPD are more likely to report a variety of physical health symptoms and are more likely to need to be hospitalized for medical reasons than those without BPD. Some of the physical health problems associated with BPD are obesity, high blood pressure, arthritis, diabetes, back pain, chronic migraines, and urinary incontinence. Lisa has all of the above.

Additionally, there are health-related lifestyle issues. Borderlines are more likely to smoke, drink alcohol, be sedentary, use sleep medication, and use pain medication. Lisa does all of those things. The link between BPD and health problems is complex, but Lisa's poor lifestyle choices seem to be a combination of a lack of motivation to do positive things for herself and using nicotine and drugs to self-medicate and try to feel better.

A study in the <u>New York Times</u> found that people with any type of mental illness are 70 percent more likely to smoke cigarettes than people without mental illness. As for substance abuse, some studies indicate that over 50 percent of borderlines abuse drugs. One explanation is that BPD and substance abuse share common pathways in the brain, and another is that borderlines simply use drugs to decrease the intense emotional experiences that are a hallmark of BPD.

Because borderlines find themselves trapped in a relentless loneliness from which the only relief comes from the physical presence of others, this often leads to bar hopping or going to other crowded haunts, which has its own disappointments and risks.

Lisa's use of crystal methamphetamine while living on the streets has had long term consequences. She developed "meth mouth," which is a term for rampant tooth decay and tooth fracture caused by the corrosive substances in crystal meth. Lisa's teeth rotted to the gum line from the effect of meth vapors on her tooth enamel. The fact that living on the street is not conducive to good dental hygiene and regular brushing did not help either.

She had all her teeth pulled when she was 29 and was fitted for dentures.

Her chronic back pain will be a lifetime issue because it stems from the hit and run accident that occurred when she was walking across the street while living on the streets. She now has three herniated disks and takes pain medication daily, in addition to quarterly steroid injections, WHEN we can find a pain doctor that accepts Medicaid. Without Medicaid, the injections would cost us $10,000 each.

Whether from her 125-pound weight gain or from all of the potent medications she has been taking all her life, Lisa's liver enzymes are dangerously elevated. She also has debilitating migraine headaches about ten days out of every month, and is on the verge of developing diabetes. Her urinary issues require the perpetual wearing of incontinence pads, which contribute to frequent urinary tract infections.

She is a thirty-year-old with the body of a sixty-year-old.

Chapter 29

Even the Drug Dealer Fired Her

Several mental and emotional illnesses occur much more frequently in people with borderline personality disorder than they do in the general population, according to recent research. In medical literature, these are called coexisting, or comorbid, conditions. Lisa has several, including bipolar disorder, major depression, and anxiety disorder.

Scientists have only been able to theorize why BPD rarely travels alone. Perhaps the personality disorder makes a person more vulnerable to the others, or maybe some of the same biological factors that lead to BPD's emotional instability also lead to other mental conditions.

Lisa's anxiety often made her virtually unable to function, and it often led to impulsive behavior in an attempt to relieve her restlessness and tension. She would respond to this vague but horrible feeling by either cutting herself or by turning to illegal drugs for distraction. She would act on impulse, even in the face of long-term negative consequences.

One somewhat benign uncontrollable impulse was her tendency to badger someone, usually me, with constant, unremitting phone calls only minutes apart, during which she would require continual reassurance. Often, I would lose my temper after the seventh or eighth call in thirty minutes, there would be a shouting match over the phone, and one or both of us would hang up on the other. Thirty minutes later, she would call and in a whining voice, apologize. By this time I was feeling guilty at impatiently mishandling the situation, and we would often both end up in tears.

Lisa's cutting episodes in response to her paralyzing anxiety had decreased over time, as she began to understand the risks involved. She really didn't want to die; she just wanted to escape the emotional pain of her anxiety. She began to realize that so many things could go wrong: she might get an infection from a dirty knife, she might cut too deep, and she might not get help in time and die.

Medicating herself with crack cocaine became the modus operandi for relieving her anxiety attacks. Unfortunately, although crack calmed her nerves immediately and significantly, it often rebounded with even stronger anxiety attacks after its effects wore off.

One day she became so desperate to escape from her "demons" that she persuaded an acquaintance from another part of town to bring her some crack. She had no money to pay him, so he took her television set and promised to keep it until she could pay him.

Over the next few days, she accumulated the $40 to pay him, but he refused to return the television. He said it was too far to drive and that she had to come and get it by the next day or he would sell it.

The constant, impulsive phone calls began—to me and to the crack guy. She begged me to drive her to his house so that she could get her television. She called him to beg him not to sell the TV. My husband and I were at a Houston Rockets basketball game, so there was no way I could drive her there that evening, even if I had wanted to. I told her that I would drive her the next day but that someone would have to go with us for protection.

"Mo-om," she patronizingly replied. "He's not a dangerous drug dealer. He's a guy I knew on the streets."

"I don't care. We are not going there alone, and if you want me to drive you to get your $300 television that you pawned for $40 worth of crack, then you are going to follow my rules."

"But we have to go tonight or he'll sell it," she insisted.

"Call him and tell him we will be there tomorrow."

"But, Mom" calls continued throughout the evening until I stopped answering the phone and just tried to enjoy the basketball game. I guess that's when she began calling the crack guy over and over, begging him not to sell her TV.

The next day, the two of us, along with her boyfriend Colt, drove to crack guy's apartment. I instructed her to tell him to bring the TV outside so that she wouldn't have to go inside his apartment. I stayed in my car, which was about 20 yards from crack guy's front door, as Lisa and her boyfriend rang the doorbell.

Crack guy handed the television set to Colt, Lisa gave crack guy the money, and a conversation ensued. I became a bit nervous as they spoke in low tones that I couldn't hear. My fingers were on the 9-1-1 numbers of my cell phone.

After what seemed like minutes but was only about thirty seconds, Lisa, Colt, and the television returned to my vehicle. I asked Lisa what the conversation had been about. She replied, "He said never to call him again for crack because I'm too much trouble."

Even the drug dealer couldn't put up with her anymore and fired her!

Chapter 30

Motorcycle Madness

It was about 8 p.m. when the call came.

"Miss Linda, this is Colt. Lisa fell off my motorcycle and is lying in the street!" he breathlessly exclaimed.

It took a moment for my brain to register what he said, but then the frantic questions started. "Is she hurt? What happened? Is she conscious?"

"A guy in the car that was behind us stopped and helped me carry her to the curb, but she is unconscious."

"Is she breathing?" I asked, afraid of the answer.

"Yes, she's moaning."

"Where are you? I'll be right over. Did you call an ambulance?"

"No, I haven't called one, but we're only a few blocks from your house."

When I arrived about two minutes later, Lisa was partially sitting up and seemed to be in a daze. I rushed to her and put my arm around her.

"Lisa, what happened?"

"With slurred speech she replied, "I fell off the back of Colt's bike."

At this point Colt interrupted. "We were coming to see you, Miss Linda, because I was worried about her."

"Why were you worried about her?"

"Well, suddenly and out of the blue, she started accusing me of wanting to leave her."

"Why? Did you say or do anything to make her think that?"

"No. I just told her that I would have to go out of town for a few days on a construction job, and she freaked out. She accused me of lying about the trip and using it as an excuse to leave her. Then she grabbed a knife on the table and started cutting her wrists. I didn't know what to do, so I dragged her to the motorcycle, made her get on, and we started heading toward your house. All of a sudden I heard a 'thump' and looked back and saw her rolling on the ground in the street. The car behind us screeched to a stop and the guy jumped out to help. "

At this point, Lisa began to complain of her body hurting all over. I made a quick decision.

I told Colt, "We need to get her to a hospital because she may have a concussion and broken bones. Rather than call an ambulance, I think it will be quicker if we just drive her there."

Colt sat in the back seat, cradling Lisa's head in his lap, as we discussed what happened. I asked why she fell off.

"I don't know. She was threatening to cut herself back at home, so maybe she was trying to kill herself by falling off," he replied tentatively.

It was a terrifying thought.

When we arrived at the emergency room, I informed the attending medical personnel about her mental illness and hesitantly added, "There is a possibility that she was trying to harm herself by falling off the bike intentionally."

Lisa overheard me and screamed, "Noooo, Mom. They will put me in restraints. I wasn't trying to kill myself! I had just taken a Xanax to calm down, and it made me so drowsy that I just fell off. That's all. I just sort of fell asleep on the bike."

The nurse promised me he would place Lisa in a private, monitored room and evaluate her for both physical injuries and suicidal ideation. He said I could not come into the room with her during the exam because she was an adult, but that I could join them after the examination.

In about thirty minutes, Colt and I were beckoned into the examining room. We were told that she had no broken bones or serious injuries, just multiple contusions that would cause her to be very sore for the next few days. He also said there was no indication that she was suicidal at this time and that she should not have been riding a motorcycle after taking a sedative. *Duh!*

Lisa was kept under observation for a few more hours, and we were released around two o'clock in the morning.

The drama didn't end there, though. A few days later, Colt was picked up by the police on an outstanding warrant and put in jail. To Lisa and to most borderlines, that was abandonment. She saw no difference between someone leaving her because they wanted to and someone leaving against their will. All she knew was that she was alone. *Again.*

Chapter 31

"Déjà vu All over Again"

--Yogi Berra, New York Yankees

Lisa had a tough time after Colt left. Once again, she felt forsaken and deserted, and I was concerned that the new young man she had begun seeing, Marcus, was simply using her to get money from me. She had recently been asking for more money than usual, claiming it was for Christmas presents for friends.

On Christmas day I sensed she was teetering on the brink of acting out. She was nervous, couldn't sit still, and didn't seem to be enjoying the day with the eight other family members that had gathered at our home. The warning signs were there, but I felt helpless. All I could do was wait for the emotional explosion, whenever it would come.

Two days later, she called and insisted that she needed some household supplies from Walmart. For me, shopping with her at Walmart ranks right up there with having a root canal or a mammogram. She wants to go down every aisle and buy everything she sees. It's like when she was a child and I had to say "no" constantly whenever we were shopping. I told her I would give her a Walmart gift card and bus fare so she could get there on her own accord. An hour later, the phone rang.

"Mom, they are going to arrest me for shoplifting," she stated with little emotion in her voice.

"What? Where are you?" I shouted, with a lot of emotion in MY voice.

"I'm at Walmart, and security caught me leaving the store with a shopping cart full of things."

"But I gave you a $50 card. Why didn't you use it?"

"I…don't…know." Now she was sobbing. "I need you to come right now and bring all my medications in their original bottles so they can see what meds I am on when I go to jail."

"Well, did you just forget to pay?" I pressed. "Tell them you have a gift card and just forgot to pay."

"I can't because everything has already been bagged, and they have me on security cameras."

That didn't make a lot of sense to me until later, when I discovered that she had brought her own used Walmart bags into the store and filled them as she shopped the aisles. When they were all filled, she tried to walk out of the store with them as if she had purchased them.

My heart racing, I gathered up her bottle of back pain pills and the four bottles of psychiatric drugs and drove the three miles to the store. A policeman, three security agents (dressed in baggy, hip hop clothes to blend in with the customers, I guess), and Lisa were all in the security office, which was about the size of a closet. Also in the "closet" was the shopping cart. It was filled with, of all things, MEN's items!

Angrily raising my voice, I demanded, "What are all these men's shorts, socks, tees, shaving cream, and razors doing in your shopping cart? Who put you up to this?"

"Marcus said he needed some things," she replied in a small voice.

"So you thought you'd STEAL them?" I was practically apoplectic. "Why didn't you use your gift card," I asked for the fifth time, and why doesn't Marcus get his own damned shorts? Did he tell you to steal these?"

She bowed her head and started to shake a bit. Her voice broke. Her eyes had filled, and the tears were starting to spill down her cheeks.

"No…I…don't…know. I didn't want to spend my gift card on him. I wanted to use it on myself."

What? She didn't want to use her gift card on him, but she was willing to steal for him? Again that borderline trait: impulsivity without thinking about consequences.

"I'm going to jail and I'm afraid of being off my meds like last time. I'm scared the voices will come back and tell me to kill myself. I don't want to be off my meds!"

She was becoming hysterical. She was more afraid of being off her meds than of jail itself. She had good reason. The last time she was in jail, she was told it would be two weeks before she would see a psychiatrist and be placed on meds.

A little bit of guilt began to creep in alongside my anger as I wondered, "If I had just taken her to Walmart myself, could this have been avoided?"

One of the security people was running the security video for the policeman, so I watched as it showed Lisa taking items off the shelves and placing them into used Walmart plastic bags in her cart so it would look as if she had already checked out. *She is such an amateur shoplifter.*

Before the policeman handcuffed her and escorted her to his car, she had to sign a form stating that she would never enter a Walmart store again. *Thus, Walmart was added to the list of stores from which she had been caught shoplifting. Let's see; that makes it Food Town, Walgreen's, Kroger, and now Walmart.*

I gave the policeman the bag with her medication, and he assured me that he would tell jail personnel she was on psychiatric medications so that she could be evaluated by a doctor as soon as possible. He added that there had recently been many improvements in the jail system regarding mentally ill patients and there was a good chance she wouldn't have to be off her meds for very long. He allowed me to give her one last dose of her medication.

As she was getting into the squad car, she begged, "Mom, please bail me out. I don't want to be off my meds. I am so scared of the voices."

I told her that everything would be okay and that I loved her. But I did not promise to bail her out. *I was surprisingly calm.*

I had been through this scene before, right in that very security office. I guess that's why I felt calmer and less emotional than I was back then. I could think more clearly and objectively because I didn't have to do my thinking through a veil of shock and disappointment.

She didn't know it yet, but I was not planning to bail her out, as I had done the last time. I was also not planning to hire a lawyer, as I had done the last time, when court appearances, pee tests, and bondsman check-ins dragged on for months. She would have to ask for a court-appointed attorney and resolve this situation herself. However, I didn't feel 100 per cent sure it was the right thing to do, given her BPD issues, so I texted her therapist, Carol.

Meanwhile, I drove to Lisa's townhome to confront and "kick out" anybody who was squatting there and mooching off her. Two young men answered the door, both of whom I was acquainted with. I told them in no uncertain terms that they would have to leave immediately.

"No problem," they both said and gathered their belongings.

"Is there anybody else in the house?"

"Yes," one of them replied. "Marcus is upstairs."

"Marcus!" I screamed, getting angry again. "Get down here now. You have to leave."

"But my pants are in the dryer downstairs."

"I don't care. Get down here right now."

The next thing I knew, Marcus was slowly and gingerly coming down the stairs. He didn't have a stitch of clothing on and was holding a hand towel over his private parts.

"Why are you naked?" At this point I was more shocked than angry.

"I told you my pants are in the dryer, and I don't have any underwear."

It was now clear why Lisa was buying underwear for him!

"Well, get your pants out of the dryer, put them on, and get out of here," I instructed. "And don't come back because Lisa isn't going to be back any time soon."

After all three guys left, as I was locking the townhome, my cell phone rang. It was Lisa's therapist, returning my call.

Trying to remain calm and comprehendible, I related to Carol what had happened. I explained my conundrum about whether I should get her out of jail, given her mental illness, or let her suffer the natural consequences.

Carol didn't hesitate in responding.

"Even though she has an illness, Lisa still knows right from wrong. She has to grow up. She knows she can't act like this, but she does anyway and always expects you to bail her out. You shouldn't do it this time."

That's all I needed to hear. It confirmed what my gut was telling me, and I knew what to do: Nothing. She would serve her time.

Chapter 32

Mental Tank Blues

Lisa seemed to be handling her arrest better than she had the last time. Maybe she wasn't as afraid because she knew what to expect. One thing was different, though. Because she was on psychiatric medications, she was now being processed differently.

The Harris County Jail is considered the largest mental institution in the state, housing over ten thousand prisoners with as many as 40% of them considered mentally ill. A few years ago, a collaborative effort among the sheriff's office, MHMRA, and the Harris County Psychiatric Center resulted in recommendations to improve the existing program.

One of the proposals created a Mental Health Unit with deputies and detention officers that were specially trained in mental health-crisis incident management. They undergo rigorous training in skills such as crisis intervention, de-escalation techniques, and suicide detection. They even wear blue polo shirts rather than patrol deputy shirts, designed to lessen confrontation with inmates. Inmates formerly housed in general-population group cells are now sent to this unit and receive a psychiatric evaluation within twenty-four hours instead of the previous two to three weeks.

Lisa was sent to the Mental Health Unit immediately upon arrival, and within nineteen hours, she was evaluated by a psychiatrist. The system wasn't perfect, however, and the jail isn't a pharmacy. She was allowed to continue taking Baclofen for her back pain but none of her four psychiatric medications. Instead, she was given Risperdal to replace all four psych meds. About four days after abruptly stopping her Xanax, Halperidol, Cogentin, and Seroquel, and according to her cellmates, she went into seizures several times.

Lisa was not the only one who was not as stressed this time about her incarceration. The humiliation and trauma I experienced a few years ago when I visited her was mitigated greatly by having a general idea of what to expect and a familiarity with the procedures. *At least that's what I thought.*

The jail's visitors' parking lot was overflowing, so I had to find a spot a couple of blocks away. As I walked toward the facility, I had to step over vomit on the sidewalk. *Probably from a mother visiting for the first time…been there, done that.*

I was early, but the waiting area was already so packed with people that I couldn't even see the signs directing visitors to the proper area. I had to keep asking people which line they were in. Nothing looked as I remembered it from the last time Lisa was here, and the visiting protocol seemed to have changed.

When I finally found the correct line for visitors to Lisa's unit and checked in with the officer, I put my purse and cell phone in a locker, and entered a long, snaking line to go through the metal detectors. There were some intriguing people in that line, including a uniformed airline pilot and a soldier in fatigues. I couldn't help but wonder whom they were there to see.

After passing through the metal detectors, the elevator took me to the third floor, where I saw the mass of people standing around, waiting for their turns with their loved ones. Nothing had changed there, and it all looked hauntingly familiar with its semi-circle of glass partitions.

Since this was only my second time as a jail visitor, I wasn't exactly the pro that I thought I was, and I was overcome by the sights and sounds of this sad and forbidding visiting room. One of the things that had not changed was the loud cacophony of voices as people shouted into the small, metallic, barred circle lodged in the thick piece of dirty glass which separated them from their loved ones. I tried to focus on and listen to one conversation—not to eavesdrop, but to avoid the dissonant sensory overload. It didn't work, and just as I thought my head would explode, Lisa entered the room on the other side of the glass partition.

She was wearing the ubiquitous, orange-is-the-new-black jumpsuit and flashed a big smile when she picked me out from among the visitors. To my surprise, she was upbeat and seemed fine. She told me about the new friends she had made and how good and protective they were of her. *Lisa has always had the uncanny knack of making friends anywhere she went.*

As we talked (yelled) through the glass, she said her back was hurting badly and that she was very sorry and had learned her lesson. She had "pretty good" cellmates and had been told that since this was her first theft charge, a class B misdemeanor, she might get a choice of one year of probation or 30-60 days in jail. She added that she would choose the jail time rather than the probation to "get it over with."

She chatted on for a few minutes about her experiences. She said she went to bed at nine and got up at seven, and that the food was horrible.

"We get some kind of grits for breakfast, a piece of baloney between two slices of bread for lunch, and some kind of nasty soup and cornbread for dinner," she said. She asked me to put some money into her jail account so she could buy some granola bars, snacks, and hygiene products.

After about fifteen minutes and although we had about five minutes left on our visiting time, she suggested that I leave so that someone else could talk. We "air kissed" through the glass, and I assured her that I would visit her once a week.

As it turned out, I didn't have to go back. When she appeared in court the next day, she was sentenced to thirty days in jail. However, because of jail overcrowding, she was given three-days-for-one credit. In other words, the thirty days became ten days. Having already spent four days in jail, she only had to serve an additional six days.

I was very surprised, and to be honest, somewhat disappointed. I had wanted Lisa to get enough of a negative jail experience to reinforce her determination not ever to return. I hoped that this ten-day incarceration would be enough to deter any future illegal acts.

When I told her brother Brian about the surprisingly short jail sentence, he wryly observed, "Even the jail wants to get rid of her."

Exactly one week after I visited, she called and said she was being released and "never, ever wanted to go back."

The repercussions of her jail time continued long after she was released. As soon as a person covered by Medicaid is incarcerated, his or her insurance benefits are immediately suspended or canceled. Normally, they are re-instated upon release. In Lisa's case, however, because she was released much earlier than expected, she had to re-apply for her insurance benefits. This process took over a month to complete.

Meanwhile, she suffered an acute gall stone attack and had to have emergency gall bladder surgery.

Most people go years and years without insurance and without any medical emergencies. Lisa can't go one month.

It took eight months of repeated submissions of her medical bills for her doctors and the hospital to obtain reimbursement. Until that finally happened, I had been "on the hook" for over ten thousand dollars.

Chapter 33

"Being a mother is an attitude, not a biological relation." –*Robert A. Heinlein*

Lisa has had great difficulty coping with her life whenever Bill and I were away from home for longer than a few days at a time. When I was at home, she would call me from fifteen to twenty times a day—no exaggeration, I have counted them—to reduce her anxiety. When I was out of the country, however, that coping skill was not available to her, and her distress and tension would build until she would lose control and submit to her harmful impulses.

On two occasions while we were on vacation, she broke into our house. The first time was in the summer of 2009 when we were in Italy with friends on an eight-day vacation trip. On about the fifth day, we received a call on in the middle of the night in our hotel room in Venice. It was my son, Brian, quickly reassuring me that everyone was all right, but then informing me that someone had broken into our home. He had received a call from our exterminator, who had in the process of spraying our back yard, encountered broken glass in the patio. He first called the police and then rang the first name that popped up in caller ID, which happened to be my son.

Immediately, our suspicions turned to Lisa. She had stolen from us on many occasions, usually from our wallets when we weren't looking, but I tried to resist believing she would take a brick and bash in the back door's window to unlock the door and get in.

Brian searched the house to determine what was missing. Nothing seemed to be gone except the bottles of Lisa's psychiatric meds. I had to accept the fact that she had stolen them in order to sell them for a street value of over five dollars per pill.

When we returned from the trip, Lisa denied everything, of course. I checked for cuts on her arms and body as evidence from the broken glass, but could find none. She maintained her innocence despite the fact that no one else could have known where I kept her pills.

At this point, I should have changed the hiding place of her medication, but I didn't. *Hindsight is 20/20.*

Two years ago, we were in Glacier Bay, Alaska, when my cell phone rang.

"Mom, it's Brian. Don't worry—everyone is okay. Your neighbor called me and said someone had broken into your house." Our neighbor was coming by to feed and walk our dog twice a day while we were away.

"What happened?" I blurted, amidst some of the most beautiful scenery in the world.

"It looks as if someone busted the sliding glass door to the patio. Glass is everywhere, and there is a lot of blood, too. Whoever broke in got cut pretty badly, it seems," Brian related calmly.

God forgive me, but my first reaction was rage, as I immediately suspected Lisa. Then I remembered the blood Brian described. My motherly instincts took over, and I began to worry about whether she had been badly cut.

The sliding glass door was immense, about seven feet by eight feet. Brian said it was shattered into millions of pieces that were strewn throughout the house and patio. As he toured the house while talking with me on his cell phone, tiptoeing among the glass fragments, he narrated what he observed.

"I can't see anything that's been stolen, but there is a trail of blood. I see blood on the carpet, on pillows, on one of your purses, on your bedspread, and yes, right up to where you keep Lisa's pills. It looks as if she has taken some. Your purse is emptied on the bed, too."

Brian secured the house and boarded up the huge, gaping opening. He and my daughter-in-law swept up as much glass as they could, but tiny glass particles still seemed to be embedded everywhere.

I was furious and determined to press charges against her. I told Brian to call the police and have them take blood samples and fingerprints so that I could press charges. I knew Lisa was the burglar, and I knew she needed to suffer the consequences of her actions. Unfortunately, the police told me later, any blood or fingerprints could be explained by the fact that she had been in the house on many occasions. I still wanted to know, though, if anyone had assisted her. Perhaps their prints would show up.

The police found no fingerprints except for Lisa's, and they took my purse to secure blood evidence. I have called the police station on numerous occasions, and the purse is still in police custody and hasn't been tested. That was two years ago.

Lisa's remorse—or maybe it was fear of jail—got the better of her, and she admitted to the break-in. She said she took a claw hammer from her tool kit and rode the city bus to my house. She insisted that she did it alone and that Colt, who was living with her at the time, tried to stop her. She didn't expect the entire door to shatter when she struck it with the hammer, though, and she panicked when she cut herself so badly. She looked for money but found none, so she took some of her pills, used a towel from my bathroom to stop the bleeding on her arm, and then quickly returned to her home via the bus. She left the hammer behind, which I later found in some bushes in the back yard.

"I couldn't control it, Mom," she quietly said, looking down.

She was remorseful and said she knew what she did was wrong but her anxiety was so strong that she had not been able to resist the impulse.

I thought long and hard about how to make Lisa take responsibility for her actions in the form of natural consequences. As I was staring at a shiny fleck of glass in one of my rugs, it hit me. The next day, I made Lisa get on her hands and knees and pick up what seemed like millions of tiny rounds of glass that had embedded in my carpeting, in my hardwood floors, and among the indentations on the aggregate stone patio. It took her many hours over several days because I wouldn't let her stop until every last particle was taken up.

And yes, the pills are now hidden somewhere else.

Chapter 34

Bubba

Lisa has been an animal lover and advocate her entire life and grew up with dogs, fish, turtles, hamsters, ferrets, and cats as pets. While she was living on the streets of Houston, she rescued Lady, a homeless, mixed-breed puppy from some kids who were throwing rocks at the tied-up dog. After moving into her townhome, she acquired two more dogs, a Jack Russell terrier puppy and a year-old pit bull named Bubba. It didn't take long for the townhome association to discover her menagerie and fine us for violating the bylaws restricting each unit to one pet, with a weight limit of fifty pounds. Both Lady and Bubba each weighed over sixty pounds.

Lisa and I appeared before the association board of directors and asked them to grant a reasonable accommodation, or exception, noting that other residents in the complex owned more than one pet. I really wasn't surprised that they denied our request, given the tumultuous history I had with them. They did agree that she could keep whichever of the three dogs she wanted, even if she chose one of the larger dogs. Unfortunately, I didn't get that agreement in writing, and it would come back to haunt us.

She tearfully but logically made the decision of which dog to keep. She had a friend who would take the Jack Russell, so that left the lovable Lady, who had been Lisa's companion since her days on the street, and the much-younger pit bull, Bubba. She chose to keep Bubba for two reasons. Bill and I were willing to adopt Lady, plus Bubba was much younger. Lisa said she loved Lady so much that she couldn't bear to watch Lady grow old and die. Additionally, because Lady would be living with Bill and me, Lisa could visit her often.

At first the decision worked out beautifully. Lisa was happy with Bubba and trained him well. He was a comfort to her when she was upset and would lick her tears when she cried. He had a knack for knowing when she needed comfort and would snuggle as close to her as he could. He showed none of the aggressive tendencies that some dogs of his breed have been castigated for, and he was gentle and loving with children as well as adults. He became her emotional support dog, and we registered him as such with the National Service Animal Registry. Lady, too, thrived with us and led a life of ease. We adored her.

Fast forward four years. We received a letter from the association's attorney saying Bubba was a "dangerous breed" and would have to be removed. According to the attorney's letter, we had thirty days to remove the dog from the premises or it would be taken by authorities.

Needless to say, Lisa was hysterical. I was afraid her reaction to this emotional crisis would be to self-harm or do something else destructive, so I was determined that Lisa would keep her pet even if it meant another fight with the board. Friends and family on Facebook overwhelmingly supported us with ideas and strategies to present to the board. One even provided me with the telephone number of a local television reporter who might be willing to "expose a townhome association that was trying to take away a disabled person's therapy dog."

I met with the board, and I reminded the members that they had told us years ago that Lisa could keep any of the three dogs—even the pit bull. Unfortunately, they developed a sudden case of amnesia and denied ever saying that. They refused to talk about the issue further and instructed me to talk to their attorney. I was livid, but I had no written proof. I left the meeting so angry that I was actually dizzy.

On my drive home, after consoling Lisa and promising her that this was not over, I wracked my brain to recall if any other homeowners had been at that meeting four years earlier and had heard the board tell Lisa she could keep any one dog. Fortunately, I remembered the names of two people who had attended. They agreed to help us, so I carefully crafted a letter to the attorney. I reminded the attorney that Lisa was disabled and protected under the Americans with Disabilities Act and that I could provide two witnesses who heard the board give Lisa permission to keep any dog she chose. I also asked them to remove the $600 for legal fees the association had charged me in this matter.

I never received a response. I did, however, about two weeks later, get a notice in the mail from the property manager that the $600 we had been charged for legal fees had been removed. I can only surmise that the attorney advised the board to drop the matter.

The story does not have a happy ending, however. About a year later, in January of 2015, when Bubba was six years old, he developed swelling around his neck and groin. The veterinarian had a grave expression on his face as he gave us the devastating news. Bubba had cancer, a progressive lymphoma. He had only about three months to live because there is no effective treatment for this disease in dogs. Large doses of expensive chemotherapy can prolong life in about 85% of cases, but only for about a year. Again fearful of Lisa's reactions to losing him, I promised to try to keep him alive as long as possible and allowed the vet to treat Bubba. Tragically, he was one of those dogs in the 15% that did not respond, and he died approximately four months after diagnosis.

The cruel irony is that Lisa had chosen to keep Bubba because he was likely to live longer than Lady, who was seven years his senior. At the time of Bubba's untimely death, Lady was still going strong at thirteen years of age.

Of course, Lisa was devastated over this traumatic loss. Coming to terms with the loss of a beloved pet is difficult for anyone, and it is magnified many times for someone with BPD, as intense feelings of abandonment are often triggered. Her therapist was invaluable in helping Lisa cope with her agonizing pain, and she remarked that Lisa had come a long way. Instead of cutting herself to mask her grief, she faced her pain by being aware of her feelings, not scared of them.

Her crying episodes still occur but they are spaced farther apart. That seems to be her way of handling her pain—spreading it out over time. Sometimes emotional pain can be managed far better if experienced over time in tolerable increments and not confronted all at once.

Chapter 35

"Success is how high you bounce
when you hit bottom." *–Gen. George S. Patton*

Lisa is 33 years old now. She has not had a suicide attempt or any type of self-harming episode in the past two years, not even after the death of her dog. She hasn't been in jail, nor has she stolen anything (to my knowledge). She has surrounded herself with friends who are solid citizens and don't do drugs. She takes her medication regularly, has worked hard on her therapy, and has a wonderful therapist who has helped her develop coping skills for her self-destructive emotions.

Some of the activities she uses to self-soothe are listening to music, taking her dog for a walk, going for a swim, calling a friend, bathing her dog, looking at Facebook, watching television, scrapbooking, coloring her hair, coloring in a child's coloring book (the new fad these days), punching a pillow, and a long list of others. Her brother Brian came up with a good one: hugging her dog. That's her favorite, and it was Bubba's, too.

Lisa has a new dog now. It took awhile because she felt she didn't want to be disloyal to Bubba, but Maximilliam, also a rescue pet, has won her heart. Max is a Welsh Corgi-Labrador retriever mix (*envision that!*) who is less than a year old, so she has a chance, with her animal training skills and special way with animals, to teach him to be a loving companion.

Violation notices from the townhome association are few and far between now, and I believe Lisa will soon be responsible enough to manage her own medications. Her family even gets Christmas and birthday cards and gifts from her now, something she never thought to do for many years.

I have also accomplished something major that has helped both of us, which is learning and applying the skill of validation that I learned in the Family Connections course. I have learned to listen instead of argue and criticize. I don't try to make her feelings go away; instead, I accept her feelings because no matter how ridiculous they seem to me, they are real to her. I don't necessarily agree; I just try to empathize so that she can feel less lonely and different. Sometimes, validating her feelings is like turning off a switch because she calms down so quickly. Am I perfect? No. There are times I fail miserably.

I have even learned to recognize early signs of irritability or potential conflict and intervene before her rational thinking skills break down and she goes into a full-blown rage. But, most importantly I make sure that her angry outbursts never work so that she knows that she will never get what she wants by angry, even violent reactions. Even if safety is a concern because of threat of injury to herself or others, I know to call the police or ambulance and disengage.

She still has the rare transient psychotic episode, but an episode usually only arises when she hasn't taken her anti-psychotic medication. As is the problem with many people taking such medication, she doesn't like the way it makes her feel—drowsy, sluggish, slow-thinking—so there are times when she skips doses. When she starts hearing voices, though, she knows she needs to take it.

My daughter still has an obsession with money. She seems to have a fear of being without money. She says it stems from her days on the streets when she had to beg on street corners. She constantly tries to manipulate me into giving her extra money by creatively inventing stories: going out of town with a friend, need toilet paper, need hygiene products, dog is out of food. We have an allowance schedule, however, and I try to stick with that despite her pleadings of needing food or whatever emergency reason she comes up with.

Her anxiety causes her to call me many times a day, often as many as ten or twelve. She has to tell me when she stubs her toe, when she feels bad, when she feels good, when her tummy hurts, when she has misplaced something, when her head hurts, when it is thundering, when the dog has a cut, when she can't find her shoes, etc., etc. It is maddening sometimes, but it sure is better than a few years ago when she would call me in either a borderline rage or depression with a knife to her wrists.

If I just don't have time to talk to her or just don't want to, I tell her so, lovingly and calmly. Or, I may ask her not to call for the next two hours because I want a rest. In the past, she might have reacted angrily, feeling hurt and rejected. Now she understands and tries to comply with my requests.

It really has gotten much better.

Epilogue

"Guilt to motherhood is like grapes to wine."

–Fay Weldon

Watching a loved one suffer from borderline personality disorder is painful, frightening, and confusing. Since by the very nature of the illness, the symptoms appear and disappear erratically, you never know what to expect.

I have experienced a wide range of conflicting feelings and emotions, from denial to anger to shame to guilt to hope and to hopelessness, wondering why my life couldn't have been as normal as my friends' lives were. I dreaded the ringing of the phone, just as many relatives of people with a mental illness grow to do. After all, "no news is good news," right?

There has also been enormous sadness. I cried a lot, but I also carried my pain inside. I felt the tragedy of having the life of my daughter devastated, and I saw my child's life becoming so much less than I wanted. Frustration and anger came from the helplessness I felt in my inability to lessen the symptoms of the illness. My motherly instincts and role as a parent were slowly eroded.

The people closest to a person with borderline personality disorder, whether it is a parent, spouse, sibling, or friend, bear the brunt of their erratic behaviors. To make matters worse, there is little information available to help them understand and deal with the loved ones who experience extreme mood swings, dangerous impulsivity, and tumultuous relationships. Trying to cope leaves families feeling confused, frustrated, helpless, angry, and lonely. Families might become so angry and critical of their loved one that they chase the person with BPD away; or they might back off completely, cringing in fear of causing another outburst or disruption; or they might become total enablers, taking complete care of the person with BPD. *Or all three in a never-ending roller coaster ride.*

Families need support. No family should cope with a person with BPD in isolation. The support of other families and spouses facing similar pain and problems can transform the frustration and self-blame of the borderline's family members when they realize they are not the only ones facing these problems. Family support groups and classes sponsored by The National Alliance on Mental Illness (NAMI) and The National Education Alliance for Borderline Personality Disorder (NEA-BPD) are located throughout the country.

210

The NAMI Family-to-Family Education Program is free for family members, partners and significant others with major depression, bipolar disorder, schizophrenia, borderline personality disorder, panic disorder, obsessive-compulsive disorder, addictive disorders, and other co-occurring brain disorders.

The course is a series of twelve weekly classes structured to help caregivers understand and support individuals with serious mental illness while maintaining their own well being. The course is taught by a team of trained NAMI family member volunteers who know what it's like to have a loved one struggling with one of these brain disorders. There is no cost to participate in the program, and over 150,000 people in North America have completed this course.

The NEA-BPD Family Connections course is designed specifically for parents, spouses, adult children, and siblings of individuals with borderline personality disorder. These family members develop skills that will be helpful to them for their own well being and build a support network with other individuals who have a borderline loved one.

The course content of Family Connections was developed by two practicing clinician/researchers and allows group participants to obtain current information about BPD and the latest research, acquire and practice the application of coping skills based on dialectical behavior therapy, enjoy an open and supportive forum for discussion, and develop a support network. Group leaders are family members of borderlines and have been trained to maintain the integrity of the program.

Research data documents that the family members who have participated in the Family Connections course experience a decrease in depression, burden, and grief, and gain an increase in empowerment. I certainly concur with those data. Having a supportive place to talk and learn about BPD was and continues to be indispensable to the mental health of both my daughter and me.

Through my support group for family members of borderlines, I discovered that my feelings were actually part of the natural grieving process and are typical reactions to any major loss. It was through my support group that I learned about the Family Connections course. My husband and I were so grateful for the skills we learned that we went on to become certified instructors. We also learned that the two most successful treatments used to help treat people with BPD are Dialectical Behavior Therapy (DBT) and medication.

DBT was developed by Dr. Marsha Linehan and her colleagues at the University of Washington. DBT is a form of cognitive behavioral therapy (CBT), but is highly specific and aggressive and has shown to be an effective form of therapy in treating borderlines. The program is called "dialectical" because of the paradoxes in treating borderlines. On one hand, the borderline must accept his illness and himself while, on the other hand, he or she must be working to change. Resolving these seemingly contradictory efforts is how the therapeutic process moves forward.

Emotion regulation is the key element addressed by this form of therapy. It does not try to REMOVE emotion, but teaches borderlines to experience the emotions without allowing the emotions to be in control. Therapy by specialists trained in DBT techniques usually lasts a minimum of two years and includes both individual and group sessions. This treatment is costly, however, and not all insurance plans will cover the expense.

Medication alone is not effective in treating BPD overall. There is no magic pill. It is helpful, however, in working on other, comorbid issues such as depression, anxiety, and impulsivity and in helping the brain's biological chemicals to function properly. Medications such as anti-depressant, anti-anxiety, and antipsychotic drugs can help ease acute symptoms so the client is able to settle down and concentrate on treatment.

At this time there is no complete cure for the disorder; however, science has come a long way in the treatment of BPD, and numerous studies are underway. Twenty-five years ago, the illness was considered to be nearly hopeless; today with proper treatment, BPD can be managed effectively.

Recent research based on long-term studies of people with BPD suggests that, with treatment, the overwhelming majority of people will experience significant and long-lasting periods of reduction in symptoms and improvement in their lives. Those who do not experience a complete recovery may nonetheless be able to live meaningful and productive lives. They probably will require some form of treatment—whether medications or psychotherapy—to help control their symptoms even decades after their initial diagnosis with borderline personality disorder.

I believe that my daughter will fall into the second group and require some form of treatment, especially for her co-existing conditions, for a long time to come. However, she has already come a long way.

Lisa and I have both reconciled with this illness.

I think we're going to make it.

APPENDICES

DIAGNOSTIC CRITERIA FOR BPD
in Children, Adolescents, and Adults

Borderline personality disorder is discussed in the *American Psychiatric Association's Diagnostic and Statistical Manual, or DSM)*, a standard reference for the diagnosis and treatment of mental illnesses. Some clinicians have believed that children cannot have BPD because a child's personality changes over time during the years between one and eighteen and has not yet "set" for life, and therefore, he or she may just be going through a phase. However, most clinicians today are certain that children can have BPD and often have symptoms that are similar to those of adult with BPD. As with adults, the symptoms are severe, intense, and persistent.

There is no single medical test to diagnose BPD, and a diagnosis is not based on one sign or symptom. A valid diagnosis involves an extensive assessment by a psychologist or psychiatrist after a comprehensive psychiatric interview as well as talking with previous clinicians, medical evaluations, and interviews with friends and family. To be diagnosed with BPD, a person must have at least <u>five</u> of the nine symptoms discussed below.

1. **AN EXTREME FEAR OF ABANDONMENT ACCOMPANIED BY DESPERATE BEHAVIORS DESIGNED TO PREVENT IT.** Young children might excessively cling to parents; in adolescence, it may result in clinging to boyfriends or girlfriends, which may result in using threats to harm themselves to prevent the friend from even briefly leaving them. In adults something as simple as a business trip by a spouse can trigger intense, uncontrollable feelings of abandonment. In their book *Stop Walking on Eggshells,* Mason and Kreger articulate the fear of abandonment experienced by someone with BPD: "Imagine the terror that you would feel if you were a seven-year-old, lost and alone in the middle of Times Square in New York City. Your mom was there a second ago, holding your hand. Suddenly the crowd swept her away, and you can't see her anymore. You look around frantically, trying to find her. Menacing strangers glare back at you. This is how people with BPD feel nearly all the time."

2. **A PATTERN OF INTENSE, UNSTABLE RELATIONSHIPS.** Most of us see good and bad qualities in other people, but borderlines cannot hold both positive and negative images in their brains at the same time. People are seen as either good or evil, either for me or against me. This is a common borderline defense mechanism called "splitting." Borderlines have trouble maintaining relationships due to such extremes of affection and dislike. Relationships begin quickly and become intensely close very quickly. Then they go badly just as quickly. Adolescents have trouble with boyfriends and girlfriends, and adults have difficulty with significant others, children, co-workers, and employers. A minor disagreement can turn into a big fight, resulting in the borderline's intense loathing of the other and possible loss of control and subsequent violence. Children may place people such as parents, teachers, counselors, therapists, and friends on a pedestal and see them too important to live without. Yet, these adoring feelings can turn on a dime and result in intense feelings of hatred. Borderline children may even alternate periods of inappropriate outgoing

interactions with periods of being withdrawn and aloof.

3. **POOR AND UNSTABLE SENSE OF SELF.**
Borderlines—children, teens, and adults—don't know who they are and thus act like whomever they are with. Their senses of identity are so shaky that they rely on someone else to define their egos, and they adopt the values, habits, mannerisms, and attitudes of people they spend time with. They have emptiness in themselves that only other people can fill in their endless quest for identity. In children and adolescents with BPD, this severe uncertainty of one's identity causes great mental pain and suffering as they search for who they are. Teens might turn to gangs for acceptance, experiment with their sexuality, or block the pain with drugs.

4. **HIGH IMPULSIVITY IN SELF-DAMAGING BEHAVIORS:** spending money recklessly, shoplifting, sexual promiscuity, substance abuse, reckless driving, binge eating, bulimia, uncontrolled gambling, speeding, violent and aggressive acts. Although the examples listed are adult behaviors, borderline children are also prone to unsafe activity because they cannot distinguish between fantasy

and reality. They often have difficulty connecting behavior and consequences in the impulsivity of the moment. Even if they are aware of consequences, they might not care because the consequences will happen "sometime" in the future. All they care about is "the moment." In adolescents this impulsivity can be very dangerous. To teens with BPD, any other feeling is preferable to the intense, unbearable pain they feel in their minds. Alcohol and drugs block out that pain for awhile.

5. **SUICIDAL OR SELF-MUTILATING BEHAVIORS.** Recurrent suicidal attempts or threats and self-injurious behaviors are the hallmark of borderlines. Suicide is now the number two cause of death in adolescents, after accidents. Children as young as five or six have made serious attempts to take their own lives by jumping or taking overdoses of pills. Borderlines sometimes believe that their lives are unbearable and that death is the only escape. Self-destructive acts such as cutting or burning themselves often start in early adolescence, are most common among teenage girls, and are usually precipitated by threats of rejection by a boyfriend or girlfriend. Extreme

tattooing and multiple piercings can also be a type of self-harm.

6. **EMOTIONAL INSTABILITY AND INTENSE MOOD SWINGS THAT CAN BE EXTREME AND SHORT IN LENGTH (LASTING A FEW HOURS).** A borderline's extreme reactivity to stress, especially relationship issues, is portrayed by intense depression, unrest, anger, panic, or despair that lasts a few hours— instead of days as in bi-polar disorder. These severe mood swings can occur several times a day. For the person with BPD, it is not uncommon for feelings to swing from thrilled and excited to suicidally depressed in the space of a few hours. Many people with BPD feel so overwhelmed by their intense emotional shifts that they engage in impulsive behaviors such as self-harm in order to feel better. As for teenagers, the term "intense mood swings" practically defines adolescence. However, BPD mood swings are much more extreme and set off by minor incidents that might not trouble a more typical child. Children with BPD act out and might threaten to cut themselves whenever another child in the family receives more attention or when they learn that they have not been invited to another

child's birthday party. For borderlines of all ages, their feelings, rather than the facts, define their reality. A small hurt becomes a big deal in their eyes.

7. **CHRONIC FEELINGS OF EMPTINESS.** People with BPD feel as if they have a black hole of emptiness they cannot fill. They describe their emotionally painful experience with words such as "nothingness" and "hollowness." They feel that nothing is worthwhile or important. Children and teens with BPD find this abstract feeling difficult to describe but often say they do not feel complete, as though something is always missing. In adults, this sense of emptiness is often accompanied by feelings of boredom and loneliness, which in turn may lead to dissatisfaction with their lives and the people in their lives. They might be prone to change friends or jobs and even have brief romantic affairs to temporarily relieve the emptiness. However, the empty feelings soon return, in addition to guilt and remorse for their behavior.

8. **INTENSE AND INAPPROPRIATE FLASHES OF ANGER.** This trait usually manifests itself the same way in children, teens, and

223

adults: fits of extreme rage with little or no provocation. Most children have temper tantrums, but after fifteen or twenty minutes they usually calm down. For the borderline child the rage may continue at full intensity for hours. Adults may feel irritable and angry much of the time, and even the most trivial incident can result in an angry outburst that he or she cannot seem to control. They may hold on to their anger long after the event or threat has passed. The borderline may say and do things that are very destructive and later regret they did so, feeling shame and guilt.

9. **FEELING REMOVED FROM REALITY.**
Periods of feeling removed from reality, also called dissociation, result in the person doing things that he or she does not realize or remember. This might include brief paranoid experiences as well as episodes of feeling numb, disconnected, or unrealistically self-conscious. They may experience loss of awareness, time, location, or identity. These are usually in response to extreme stress and are of a short duration (at most, a few days). Brief episodes of paranoid thinking may occur when borderlines falsely believe that others are "out to get them." In some cases, people with BPD may

experience transient hallucinations, such as hearing strange voices or sounds. Some children may use dissociation as a coping mechanism, especially if they have been emotionally, sexually, or physically abused. This coping device can become deeply ingrained and can later interfere with functioning

Source: *Diagnostic and Statistical Manual of Mental Disorders,* Fifth Edition. American Psychiatric Association, Washington, D.C.

APPENDIX II

Resources

There is an urgent need for factual information on borderline personality disorder for people with the disorder, for their families and friends, and for health care professionals who treat patients with the disorder. Until recently, information about BPD has not been widely distributed or commonly known. Even health care workers and clinicians are not as aware of this disorder as they are of other illnesses, and an accurate diagnosis can be missed, resulting in ineffective treatment.

Twenty years ago, when I needed information about the illness, there was nothing available. Now there are hundreds of books and numerous Web articles; yet, information about BPD still lags behind the other mental illnesses. For example, schizophrenia, which affects far fewer people than BPD, is the subject of over one million books. An online search of schizophrenia results in over 32 million websites.

Many people with BPD don't understand that their symptoms and problems are the result of a bona fide medical condition and not personal or character deficiencies. Educational programs, materials, and resources provide knowledge of the disorder, its symptoms, causes, and treatments, which can make a big difference in quality of life and help them make well-informed decisions.

I have carefully vetted and scrutinized the following resources to ensure their contributory value to BPD consumers, family members, and professionals.

BOOKS FOR CONSUMERS

Aguirre, Blaise, M.D. *Borderline Personality Disorder in Adolescents.* (2014).

> This second edition of *Borderline Personality Disorder in Adolescents* offers parents, caregivers, and adolescents themselves a complete understanding of this complex and tough-to-treat disorder. It is a comprehensive guide which thoroughly explains what BPD is and what a patient's treatment options are, including an overview of the revolutionary new treatment called dialectical behavior therapy. Readers will also hear from BPD adolescents and parents who have learned how to make the best of the cards they have been dealt.

Aguirre, Blaise, M.D. and Gillian Galen, Ph.D. *Mindfulness for Borderline Personality Disorder: Relieve Your Suffering Using the Core Skill of Dialectical Behavior Therapy.* (2013).

> Expanding on the core skill of dialectical behavior therapy (DBT), this book helps the borderline reader to

target and successfully manage many of the familiar symptoms of BPD. The basics of mindfulness are learned through specific exercises.

Aron, Elaine. *The Highly Sensitive Person: How to Thrive when the World Overwhelms You.* (1997).

A psychotherapist shows you how to identify this trait in yourself and make the most of it in everyday situations. Drawing on her many years of research and hundreds of interviews, she shows how you can better understand yourself and your trait to create a fuller, richer life.

Beattie, Melody. *Codependent No More.* (1987).

This book has sold over eight million copies and was the first "big book" on the subject of diagnosing and treating codependence, which, in the author's view, is a toxic enmeshment in someone else's life, often under the guise of "helping."

Beattie, Melody. *A Reason to Live.* (1991).

This book offers responsible, practical alternatives and resources to the person considering suicide.

Blauner, Susan Rose. *How I Stayed Alive When My Brain Was Trying to Kill Me: One Person's Guide to Suicide Prevention.* (2002).

The author presents a message of hope and a program of action for the millions of people who are suicidal.

She has been through it, and she speaks and writes eloquently about feelings and fantasies surrounding suicide.

Bockian, Neal and Valerie Porr. *New Hope for People with Borderline Personality Disorder.* (2002).

Inside is a compassionate and complete look at the most up-to-date information on managing the symptoms of BPD as well as coping strategies for you, your friends, and your loved ones.

Bradshaw, John. *Healing the Shame that Binds You.* (1988).

Toxic shame limits the development of self esteem and causes anxiety and depression; it limits our ability to be connected in relationships. The author shares his own journey in healing shame.

Burch, Linda. *Growing Up Borderline: A Mother's Memoir.* (2013).

This is a candid, compelling look at one family's journey through mental illness. With heartfelt honesty and in readable style, the author gives detailed insight into the disorienting world of borderline personality disorder from her child's infancy until the age of eighteen.

Burch, Linda. *Living Borderline: A Mother's Memoir.* (2016).

In the sequel to *Growing Up Borderline,* the author describes her daughter's survival with BPD into adulthood. She also provides a list of resources for families and clinicians.

Cauwels, Janice. *Imbroglio: Rising to the Challenges of Borderline Personality Disorder.* (1992).

At 400 pages, this is not a casual read; however, it portrays with dignity and humility the suffering of those with BPD.

Chapman, Alex and Kim Gratz. *The Borderline Personality Disorder Survival Guide: Everything You Need to Know about Living with BPD.* (2007).

The book offers a complete overview of BPD, its symptoms and treatment, and ways BPD sufferers can navigate their lives with this complicated condition.

Coffey, Helen Cochran. *Don't Let Anyone Know—A Story about Mental Illness—The World Viewed Only the Silhouette!* (2012).

Heather was a young mother of two who, on the outside, looked as if she had it all. Yet, on the inside she was the victim of undiagnosed and untreated BPD, which controlled her life. The book is written by Heather's mother and conveys the chaos, devastation, and heartbreak the victims of mental illness and their families suffer.

Dolecki, Constance M. *The Everything Guide to Borderline Personality Disorder.* (2012).

This professional yet compassionate guide helps readers understand the tumultuous world of BPD, offering information on causes of BPD, warning signs from an early age, monitoring extreme symptoms, different treatment options and therapies, and maintaining safety in a relationship that involves BPD.

Elliott, Charles and Laura Smith. *Borderline Personality Disorder for Dummies.* (2009).

The comprehensive information in this volume of the "…for Dummies" series is a clear and easy guide to the symptoms, causes, and treatment of BPD. It is also filled with information to help spouses, parents, and other loved ones understand and accept the disease.

Ellis, Thomas, Psy.D. and Cory Newman, Ph.D. *Choosing to Live: How to Defeat Suicide through Cognitive Therapy.* (1996).

The authors provide tools to help readers assess the risk and understand the factors that reinforce suicidal talk and behaviors. A step-by-step program for change shows how to replace negative beliefs and develop alternative skills for solving problems.

Friedel, Robert O. *Borderline Personality Disorder Demystified.* (2004).

A comprehensive, useful, and supportive guide by a leading expert in BPD and a pioneer in its treatment, the author explains the much-misunderstood disorder and offers not only information, but hope with new effective treatments.

Fjelstad, Margalis. *Stop Caretaking the Borderline or Narcissist: How to End the Drama and Get on with Life.* (2014).

Margalis Flelstad describes how people get into caretaker roles with borderlines or narcissists and how they can get out. Caretakers give up their sense of themselves and become who and what the borderline or narcissist needs them to be. The book describes how to get out of destructive interactions and how to take new, more effective actions to focus on personal wants and needs while allowing the borderlines or narcissists to take care of themselves.

Griffith, Winter. *The Complete Guide to Prescription and Nonprescription Drugs.* (2013).

This best-selling drug reference book features over 7,000 brand and generic names with information on dangerous interactions and side effects, warnings and data for safe use, and current information on FDA reports.

Green, Tami. *Helping Someone You Love Recover from Borderline Personality Disorder (Finally and Completely).* (2008).

Tami Green is making as part of her own recovery the helping of other people to learn about BPD. She coaches the reader through the recovery process and suggests healthy approaches to managing symptoms.

Green, Tami. *Self-help for Managing the Symptoms of Borderline Personality Disorder.* (2008).

Tami Green was diagnosed with Borderline Personality Disorder. Rather than hide her mental health problem or deny it and refuse treatment as so many with BPD do, she's taken on the challenge of recovering from BPD head-on.

Gunderson, John, M.D. *Borderline Personality Disorder—A Clinical Guide.* (2008).

Dr. Gunderson provides a comprehensive guide to the diagnosis and treatment of borderline personality disorder (BPD). The second edition includes new research about BPD's relationship to other disorders and up-to-date descriptions of empirically validated treatments, including cognitive-behavioral and psychodynamic approaches. Compelling new research also indicates a much better prognosis for BPD than previously known.

Gunderson, John and Perry Hoffman (editors). *Understanding and Treating Borderline Personality Disorder: An Update for Professionals and Families.* (2005).

The editors of this practical text have brought together the wide-ranging and updated perspectives of fifteen recognized experts, who offer the hope that partnerships between mental health professionals and families of borderlines can advance our understanding and treatment of this disease.

Hall, Karyn, Ph.D. *The Emotionally Sensitive Person.* (2014).

A psychologist provides proven-effective cognitive behavioral and mindfulness techniques to help people who struggle with intense emotions. Readers are provided with evidence-based strategies for taking charge of their emotions—whether it's at home, at work, or in relationships.

Hall, Karyn, Ph.D. and Melissa Cook. *The Power of Validation: Arming Your Child against Bullying, Peer Pressure, Addiction, Self-Harm, and Out-of-Control Emotions.* (2011).

What is validation? It's "the recognition and acceptance that your child has feelings and thoughts that are true and real to him regardless of logic or whether it makes sense to anyone else," the authors write, but it doesn't mean giving in to their demands or necessarily agreeing with their feelings. This is a valuable resource for parents seeking practical skills for validating their child's feelings without condoning tantrums, selfishness, or out-of-control behavior.

Harvey, Pat and Jeanine Penzo. *Parenting a Child Who Has Intense Emotions: DBT Skills to Help Your Child Regulate Emotional Outbursts and Aggressive Behaviors.* (2009).

> This is a guide to de-escalating your child's emotions and re-directing his expressions of feelings in productive ways. Strategies are drawn from dialectical behavior therapy.

Hendrix, Harville, Ph.D. *Keeping the Love You Find.* (1992).

> This book's title may make it sound cheesy, but by helping you understand more about yourself, you will understand what you need in a relationship. Be willing to do some soul searching.

Katherine, Anne. *Boundaries: Where You End and I Begin.* (1993).

> The book helps us recognize and set healthy boundaries that bring order to our lives, strengthen our relationships, and are essential to our mental and physical health. Real-life stories illustrate the ill effects of not setting limits and the benefits gained by respecting our own boundaries and those of others.

Komrad, Mark S., M.D. *You Need Help!—A Step-by-step Plan to Convince a Loved One to Get Counseling.* (2012).

> Through a rich combination of user-friendly tools and real-life stories, Mark S. Komrad, M.D., offers step-by-step guidance and support as you take the courageous

step of helping a friend who might not even recognize that he or she is in need. He guides you in developing a strong course of action, starting by determining when professional help is needed, then moves you through the steps of picking the right time, making the first approach, gathering allies, selecting the right professional, and supporting friends or relatives as they go through the necessary therapeutic process to resolve their problems. Included are scripts based on Komrad's work with his own patients, designed to help you anticipate next steps and arm you with the tools to respond constructively and compassionately. You will also find the guidance and information needed to understand mental illness and get past the stigma still associated with it, so you can engage and support your loved one with insight and compassion in his or her journey toward emotional stability and health.

Krawitz, Roy, M.D. and Wendy Jackson. *Borderline Personality Disorder (The Facts)*. (2008).

This is a user-friendly resource co-written by a psychiatrist and a woman who has recovered from BPD.

Kreger, Randi. *The Essential Guide to Borderline Personality Disorder*. (2008).

Readers get straight-forward tools to get off the emotional roller coaster and repair relationships with loved ones who have BPD. Kreger answers questions family members most want answered: symptoms and treatment, why BPD is so misdiagnosed, complications, and associated addictions. She outlines how families can set boundaries and communicate differently to help themselves and their loved ones cope.

Kreger, Randi and Paul Mason. *Stop Walking on Eggshells: Taking your Life Back When Someone You Care About Has Borderline Personality Disorder.* (2010).

Friends and family members of borderlines are helped to understand this destructive disorder, set boundaries, and help their loved ones stop relying on dangerous behaviors. The fully revised edition has been updated with the latest research.

Kreisman, Jerold, M.D. *I Hate You, Don't Leave Me: Understanding the Borderline Personality.* (2010).

This is the new edition of the original guide to BPD published in 1989. It reflects the most up-to-date research of the disorder as well as connections between BPD and substance abuse, sexual abuse, PTSD, ADHD, and eating disorders.

Kreisman, Jerold, M.D. and Harold Straus. *Sometimes I Act Crazy—Living with Borderline Personality Disorder.* (2004).

In this source of hope, expert advice, and guidance for people with borderline personality disorder and those who love them, the authors also tell personal stories of BPD sufferers. There are sections in each chapter called Action Steps that gave borderlines a "road map" for coping and seeking help.

Lawson, Christine. *Understanding the Borderline Mother: Helping Her Children Transcend the Intense, Unpredictable, and Volatile Relationship.* (2002).

The first love in our lives is our mother. Recognizing her face, her voice, the meaning of her moods, and her facial expressions is crucial to survival. Dr. Lawson vividly describes how mothers who suffer from BPD produce children who may flounder in life, even as adults. Children of borderlines are at risk for developing BPD themselves and require early intervention. The book contains specific suggestions for developing healthier relationships between mother and child.

Lerner, Harriet, Ph.D. *The Dance of Anger.* (1985).

This is a renowned classic, a guide to understanding and reducing anger in close relationships.

Manning, Shari, Ph.D. *Loving Someone with Borderline Personality Disorder: How to Keep Out-of-Control Emotions from Destroying Your Relationship.* (2011).

If you are struggling in a tumultuous relationship with someone with BPD, this might be the book for you. The author helps you understand WHY your spouse, family member, or friend has such out-of-control emotions and how to change the way you can respond. Learn to use simple strategies that can defuse crises, establish boundaries, and transform your relationship. It is science-based on dialectical behavior therapy.

Masterson, James, M.D. *The Search for the Real Self.* (1990).

The author helps readers understand the outwardly successful, charming, and powerful individuals with personality disorders who have confounded their colleagues, family, lovers, employees, and mental health professionals. He delineates false self from healthy self.

McKay, Matthew, Ph.D. *Practical DBT Exercises for Learning Mindfulness, Interpersonal Effectiveness, Emotion Regulation, and Distress Tolerance.* (2007).

A clear and effective approach to learning DBT skills, **this is the book my daughter uses**. It offers straightforward, step-by-step exercises for learning DBT concepts and putting them to work for real and lasting change. This book has been awarded the Association for Behavioral and Cognitive Therapies Self-Help Seal of Merit, an award bestowed on outstanding self-help books that incorporate

241

scientifically tested strategies for overcoming mental health difficulties.

Miller, Dusty. *Women Who Hurt Themselves: A Book of Hope and Understanding*. (1995).

> Filled with moving stories, this book focuses on women who harm themselves through self-mutilation, compulsive cosmetic surgeries, eating disorders, and other forms of chronic injury to the body.

Mondimoor, Francis, M.D. and Patrick Kelly, M.D. *Borderline Personality Disorder: New Reasons for Hope*. (2011).

> Incorporating the latest research and thinking on the disorder, two Johns Hopkins psychiatrists conceptualize it in an original way. The authors advocate a therapeutic approach incorporating compassion and optimism in the face of what is often a tumultuous disease and agree that with proper treatment, people with borderline personality disorder can enjoy long remissions and improved quality of life.

Moskowitz, Richard, M.D. *Lost in the Mirror: An Inside Look at Borderline Personality Disorder*. (1996).

> This is a gentle, non-judgmental, and supportive self-help book for people with BPD.

Nowinski, Joseph, Ph.D. *Hard to Love: Understanding and Overcoming Male Borderline Personality Disorder*. (2014).

The book addresses symptoms, causes, and treatment targeted to men suffering from BPD.

Pershall, Stacy. *Loud in the House of Myself: Memoir of a Strange Girl.* (2011).

Stacy Pershall grew up as an overly intelligent, depressed, deeply strange girl in Prairie Grove, Arkansas, population 1,000. From her days as a thirteen-year-old Jesus freak through her eventual diagnosis of bipolar disorder and borderline personality disorder, this spirited memoir chronicles Pershall's journey through hell and her struggle with the mental health care system.

Porr, Valerie. *Overcoming Borderline Personality Disorder: A Family Guide for Healing and Change.* (2010).

Ms. Porr offers families and loved ones supportive guidance and teaches effective coping behaviors and interpersonal skills. The book was the winner of the 2011 ABCT Self-Help Book Seal of Merit Award.

Reiland, Rachel. *Get Me Out of Here: My Recovery from Borderline Personality Disorder.* (2004).

A woman who has suffered from BPD and was treated using psychodynamic psychotherapy talks about her experiences.

Santoro, Joseph, Ph.D. and Ronald Cohen, Ph.D. *The Angry Heart: Overcoming Borderline and Addictive Personality Disorders.* (1997).

> This self-help guide offers a range of practical exercises and step-by-step techniques to help you come to terms with the destructive cycle of self-defeating thoughts and behaviors of your lifestyle.

Rivers, Clarence. *Borderline Personality Disorder: Enter the Mind of a Person Living with BPD!* (2014).

> After reading this book, you will perhaps be able to understand BPD and why borderlines act the way they do. With insight to their world, you may also understand why they deserve love, compassion, and understanding instead of hatred and fear.

Slater, Lauren. *Welcome to My Country.* (1996).

> A young therapist transports us into the lives of several of her patients to help us understand those who are suffering from mental and emotional distress.

Spradlin, Scott. *Don't Let Your Emotions Run Your Life: How Dialectical Behavior Therapy Can Put You in Control.* (2003).

> This is a self-help, introductory book on DBT skills training. It explains some of the fundamental concepts of DBT and provides a structured workbook format to learn and apply the information.

U.S. Department of Health and Human Services. *Borderline Personality Disorder.* (2014).

> Concrete evidence is provided that many mental, emotional, and behavioral disorders in young people are preventable, and early detection is critical. A key tenet of this report is that school-based programs can reduce problem behaviors and improve academic outcomes.

Van Gelder, Kiera. *My Recovery from Borderline Personality Disorder through Dialectical Behavior Therapy, Buddhism, and Online Dating.* (2010).

> This haunting, intimate memoir chronicles the devastating period that led to Kiera's eventual diagnosis of BPD, including suicide attempts, drug addiction, depression, self-harm, and chaotic relationships, as well as her inspirational recovery through therapy, Buddhist spirituality, and a few online dates gone wrong.

Wiseman, Cathy. *Borderine Personality: A Scriptural Perspective.* (2012).

> Sufferers of BPD face disaster in their relationships as intense fears and feelings rule their hearts and choices. This thorough study explains how God's Word can heal the havoc of BPD.

Wright, Georgiana. *Borderline Mom: A Quick and Dirty Manual of Emotional Self Defense for Children.* (2009).

> This book focuses on one group of people affected by BPD: children whose mothers are borderline. It provides the tools to take the optimal course of action if the relationship with your borderline mom is causing you pain.

BOOKS FOR PROFESSIONALS

American Psychiatric Association. *Practice Guideline for the Treatment of Patients with Borderline Personality Disorder.* (2001).

> Developed primarily by psychiatrists in active clinical practice, an updated synthesis of current scientific knowledge is presented. This volume is organized into three parts: treatment recommendations, evidence underlying these treatment recommendations, and a summary of the areas in which better research is needed.

Bateman, Anthony and Peter Fonagy. *Psychotherapy for Borderline Personality Disorder: Mentalization-Based Treatment.* (2008).

> This practical guide explains how to treat borderline patients by helping them develop mentalizing capacity within the context of an attachment relationship. It provides the practitioner with information about how to practice mentalizing treatment in day patient and out-patient settings. There is step-by-step practical

advice on the assessment of mentalizing and interpersonal relationships, how to structure treatment, the use of basic mentalizing interventions and how to apply them, as well as information on what not to do.

Becker, Dana. *Through the Looking Glass: Women and Borderline Personality Disorder.* (2009).

In a look at facts behind why the preponderance of people diagnosed with BPD are women, the author offers an emphasis on elements of female socialization as keys to understanding the development of borderline symptoms.

Bleiberg, Ethan, M.D. *Treating Personality Disorders in Children and Adolescents.* (2004).

This groundbreaking volume is one of the first to conceptualize borderline personality disorder in children and adolescents. While personality disorders traditionally have been diagnosed only in adults, youngsters with personality disorders may come across as strikingly arrogant, defiant, and manipulative, yet their demeanor typically masks devastating experiences of vulnerability and pain. Unfortunately, this volume was written before recent research that BPD is not necessarily caused by environmental factors, i.e., bad parenting, sexual abuse or other trauma, but that there is a significant genetic component to the development of the disease. The case vignettes, however, illustrate the importance of the relationship between the therapist and patient in treatment.

Dimeff, Linda, Ph.D. and Kelly Koerner, Ph.D. *Dialectical Behavior Therapy in Clinical Practice: Applications across Disorders and Settings.* (2007).

Issues in establishing and maintaining an effective DBT program are addressed, and leading contributors, including Marsha Linehan, present applications for complex problems associated with BPD, such as substance dependence, eating disorders, and suicidal behaviors.

Freeman, Arthur. Borderline Personality Disorder: *A Practitioner's Guide to Comparative Treatments.* (2007).

Through applying a variety of modalities to identify treatment goals, including selecting assessment tools, conceptualizing progression, pinpointing pitfalls, and developing techniques, diagnosing and treating BPD has created a more successful therapeutic result.

Hoffman, Perry, Ph.D. and Penny Steiner-Grossman, Ed.D. *Borderline Personality Disorder: Meeting the Challenges to Successful Treatment. (2008).*

Social workers and other mental health clinicians are provided with practical access to the knowledge necessary for effective treatment with the most current research, information, and management considerations. The text explores the latest methods and approaches to treating BPD patients and supporting their families with handy worksheets and numerous tables that present information clearly.

Judd, Patricia and Thomas McGlashan. *A Developmental Model of Borderline Personality Disorder: Understanding Variations in Course and Outcome.* (2002).

A landmark work of its time on this difficult condition, the book emphasizes a developmental approach to BPD based on an in-depth study of inpatients at Chestnut Lodge in Rockville, Maryland, during the years 1950 through 1975. The authors present four intriguing case studies to chart the etiology, long-term course, and clinical manifestations of BPD. The first resource to chart BPD over the long term in such depth, this book is a clinical resource that reads like a novel.

Koerner, Kelly, Ph.D. *Doing Dialectical Behavior Therapy: A Practical Guide.* (2012).

Filled with vivid clinical vignettes and step-by-step descriptions, this book demonstrates the nuts and bolts of DBT. It provides an accessible introduction to DBT while enabling therapists to integrate elements of this evidence-based approach into their work with emotionally dysregulated clients.

Linehan, Marsha. *Cognitive-behavioral Treatment of Borderline Personality Disorder.* (1993).

For the average clinician, individuals with borderline personality disorder (BPD) often represent the most challenging, seemingly insoluble cases. Dialectical behavioral therapy (DBT) was the first psychotherapy shown in controlled trials to be effective with BPD. This volume is the authoritative presentation of dialectical behavior therapy, Marsha M. Linehan's comprehensive, integrated approach to treating individuals with BPD.

Linehan, Marsha. *Skills Training Manual for Treating Borderline Personality Disorder, Second Edition.* (2014).

From Marsha M. Linehan, the developer of dialectical behavior therapy (DBT), this comprehensive resource provides vital tools for implementing DBT skills training. The reproducible teaching notes, handouts, and worksheets used for over two decades by hundreds of thousands of practitioners have been significantly revised and expanded to reflect important research and clinical advances. The book gives complete instructions for orienting clients to DBT.

Miller, Rathus, Linehan, and Swenson. *Dialectical Behavior Therapy with Suicidal Adolescents.* (2006).

>This highly practical book adapts the proven techniques of dialectical behavior therapy (DBT) to treatment of multi-problem adolescents at highest risk for suicidal behavior and self-injury.

Paris, Joel, editor. *Borderline Personality Disorder: Psychiatric Clinics of North America.* (2008).

>The editor of this book has carefully selected experts in a wide range of areas dealing with BPD. These include the genetics, biology, childhood experiences, and various pharmacological and psychotherapeutic treatment approaches relevant to the disorder.

Paris, Joel. *Treatment of Borderline Personality Disorder.* (2008).

>Rather than advocating a particular approach, Joel Paris examines a range of therapies and identifies the core ingredients of effective treatment. He offers specific guidance for meeting the needs of the challenging BPD population, including ways to improve diagnosis, promote emotion regulation and impulse control, maintain appropriate therapeutic boundaries, and deal with suicidality and other crises. Highly readable, practical, and humane, the book also explains the latest thinking on the causes of BPD and how it develops.

Sharp, Carla and Jennifer Tackett. *Handbook of Borderline Personality Disorder in Children and Adolescents.* (2014).

> Clinicians have long hesitated in diagnosing BPD in children and adolescents for fear of stigmatizing the child and/or confusing the normal mood shifts of adolescence with pathology. A recent upsurge in research is inspiring the field to move beyond this hesitance, and this resource reflects the current research in diagnosis and treatment of children and adolescents.

BROCHURES AND BOOKLETS

"A BPD Brief" Revised 2006. Gunderson, John, M.D.

Downloadable at
www.BorderlinePersonalityDisorder.com.

"Borderline Personality Disorder: What You Need to Know about this Medical Illness."

National Alliance on Mental Illness. 2009 brochure.

Downloadable at www.NAMI.org.

"Family Guidelines" Revised 2006. Gunderson, John M.D. and Cynthia Berkowitz, M.D.

Downloadable at
www.BorderlinePersonalityDisorder.com.

WEB RESOURCES

Do a Google search for the U.S. Department of Health and Human Services Report to Congress on Borderline Personality Disorder – 81 pages to download. Publication May, 2011. This is the most current, most detailed official document to support your recommendation of BPD for insurance, social security, and legal purposes. Become familiar with this excellent document and resources.

www.BBRfoundation.org

   Brain and Behavior Research Foundation

www.BehavioralTech.com

   DBT referral, training, and resources

www.BorderlinePersonalityBooks.com

   Reviews of new books about BPD

www.BorderlinePersonalityDisorder.com

National Alliance for BPD has conferences, publications, videos, and education courses.

www.BorderlinePersonalitySupport.com

Peer information and support

www.BorderlinePersonalityToday.com

A compendium of articles about BPD

www.BorderlinePersonalityTreatment.com

A resource for those affected by BPD

www.BorderlineResearch.org

A private foundation that conducts research on BPD

www.BPDcentral.com

Long-established, a popular site

www.BPDdemystified.com

Updates news about BPD

www.BPDed.com

A platform for researchers and clinicians

www.BPDfamily.com

World-wide support group of 75,000 members

www.BPDrecovery.com

Focuses on recovery using cognitive therapy techniques

www.BPDresourcecenter.org

Promotes BPD education and connects people to resources

www.BPDvideo.com

"If Only We Had Known," a five-part video series about borderline personality disorder with the experiences of four families who have a loved one with BPD and featuring leading experts offering explanations. These videos offer support and help to families who are living with BPD and are an excellent teaching tool for clinics, hospital staffs, and teaching institutions.

www.BPDworld.org

Support and information

http://BRTC.psych.washington.edu

Dr. Marsha Linehan's Behavioral Research and Therapy Clinics at the University of Washington

www.CarterCenter.com

The Carter Center Mental Health Program

www.DBTselfhelp.com

A service for those seeking information about DBT

www.DealingWithEmotions.com

Peer information and support

www.FDA.gov

Provides information about the safety of medications

www.healthplace.com

Videos, tests, information

www.HopeForBPD.com

Treatment navigation

www.my-borderline-personality-disorder.com

This is a website and peer-hosted chat room for those
who have BPD and others who treat/love them.

www.NAMI.org

National Alliance on Mental Illness

www.NEPDA.org

New England Personality Disorder Association

www.NIMH.NIH.gov

National Institute for Mental Health

www.NMHA.org

Mental Health America

www.psych.org

American Psychiatric Association

www.psychcentral.com/lib/living-with-borderline-personality-disorder

Introduction to BPD, tests, symptoms, treatment

www.ReThinkBPD.com

Positive articles of advocacy from professionals, family members and persons experiencing the symptoms of BPD

www.RxList.com

Important information about thousands of medications

www.SayNoToStigma.com

Blog: Menninger Clinic, Houston

www.Tara4bpd.org

Non-profit that fosters education and research into personality disorders

www.TICLLC.org

Training and consulting in treatments and programs

FILMS AND DVDs

Corso, Debbie. *Border: A Compassionate Documentary about Borderline Personality Disorder.* (2013).

> This honest and informative, 26-minute YouTube video discusses BPD through interviews.

Columbia Pictures. *Girl, Interrupted.* (1999).

> This film is based on the real-life story of Susanna Kaysen, who was hospitalized for BPD, and is rated R. It presents a somewhat simplified view of the illness.

Dawkins Productions. *If Only We Had Known: A Family Guide to Borderline Personality Disorder.* (2014).

> This 40 minute educational DVD explores several treatments specifically designed for BPD, such as dialectical behavior therapy, mentalization, and others, as well as medications prescribed for people with BPD.

Linehan, Marsha, Ph.D. *Understanding Borderline Personality Disorder.* (2006).

> This video addresses fundamental questions about the nature of BPD, its causes, and how it can effectively be treated with Dialectical Behavior Therapy (DBT). Featured are live interview sessions with questions and answers as well as segments of actual therapy sessions. The 37-minute DVD is accompanied by a 36-page manual.

Linehan, Marsha, Ph.D. *Treating Borderline Personality Disorder: The Dialectical Approach.* (2006).

> In actual therapy sessions, the film shows Dr. Linehan teaching patients the use of such skills as mindfulness, distress tolerance, interpersonal effectiveness, and emotional regulation. Vividly depicting the various stages of treatment, this program shows how DBT helps clients decrease negative behaviors and work toward personal goals. Designed for therapists, the 45-minute DVD and accompanying 36-page manual are also suitable for use in client and family education.

Matthews, Cate, posted on Huffington Post. *Why Empathy is More Powerful Than Sympathy.* (2013).

> Empathy, Brown explains, is a more powerful choice than sympathy. Empathy enables us to relate to and console those in our lives, while sympathy distances us.

Empathy, or validation, is a critical dialectical behavior therapy skill.

SMARTPHONE APPS

"Borderline and Beyond—BPD Help" is available on iTunes. It is a self-help coach to help manage your symptoms.

"Borderline Personality Disorder" is available on ITunes and on Androids. It contains information and contacts for those suffering with BPD.

"DBT Diary Card" is available on iTunes.

"DBT Self Help" is available on Androids.

"DBT Skills Coach" is available on iTunes.

"DBT 911" is in available on Androids.

"Headspace" is a course of guided meditation/mindfulness and is available on Androids.

"Healing from BPD" is available on iTunes and allows you to document your feelings with the use of diary cards.

"Mental Health Apps" is available on iTunes and combines gamification, personalization, and science to effect behavioral change.

"PocketShrink" is available on iTunes. It allows a user to gain insight into whether or not they should seek medical help.

"Safety Plan" is free, has GPS, and is an emergency plan for suicide crises. It is available on Androids and iTunes.

HOTLINES

National BPD Hotline (TARA)   888-482-7227

This organization is dedicated to helping people with
BPD and their families find accurate information
through treatment referrals, support group information,
and educational materials.

Befrienders (Help for suicidal and self-harm thoughts,
worldwide) www.befrienders.org

Befrienders Worldwide is an independent charity
established in 2012. It consists of a global network of
349 emotional support centers in 32 countries,
spanning five continents. These centers are staffed by
more than 25,000 volunteers who provide vital support
to an estimated seven million service users each year,
providing an open space for those in distress to talk
and be heard via telephone help lines, messaging, face
to face, internet chat, outreach, and local partnerships.

Samaritans Helplines Suicide Prevention

http;//samaritanshope.org

> Confidential, compassionate, and anonymous,
> Samaritans' mission is to reduce the incidence of
> suicide by alleviating despair, isolation, distress, and
> suicidal feelings 24 hours a day.

Crisis Text Line   Text "GO" to 741-741

> Free, 24-hour, and confidential, the Crisis Text Line is
> the nation's first free, 24/7 text line for people in crisis.
> Volunteer crisis counselors use a web-based platform
> to provide emotional support to texters who are
> dealing with a wide range of issues – bullying, self-
> harm, suicidal thoughts, and more. Since 2013, crisis
> counselors have processed over seven million text
> messages and have saved countless lives.

Need Help Now?   800-273-TALK

> This 24-hour hotline is available to anyone in suicidal
> crisis or emotional distress. Your call will be routed to
> the crisis center nearest you.

APPENDIX III

GLOSSARY

ALL-OR-NONE THINKING, or "splitting," or "black-and-white thinking," conceptualizes people or events in "either-or" terms, as all good or all bad.

AMYGDALA is an almond-shaped structure, part of the brain's limbic system, which plays a key role in regulating emotions and social behavior. In people who have BPD, the amygdale is overactive, resulting in big and intense emotional responses.

ANHEDONIA is the inability to experience pleasure from activities usually found enjoyable.

ANTIPSYCHOTICS are medications that target symptoms of psychosis or thought disorders.

AXIS II is a classification in the Diagnostic and Statistical Manual-IV for personality disorders and mental retardation.

Because these are considered long-term, chronic conditions (and not acute conditions as in Axis I), insurers often fail to reimburse for treatments. The DSM-5 has shifted to a single-axis system that removes the arbitrary boundaries between mental illnesses, given that there is no fundamental difference between Axis I and Axis II disorders.

BI-POLAR DISORDER is also known as manic-depressive disorder and is known for alternating periods of depression and mania that lasts from days to months. Bi-polar disorder is effectively managed with medication.

BORDERLINE PERSONALITY DISORDER (BPD) is a serious and complex disorder affecting an estimated one to two per cent of the general population. The core symptoms common to most people with BPD are impulsive behavior, the inability to control mood or feelings, and disturbed, unstable relationships with others.

COGNITIVE pertains to thinking and mental processes such as knowing, perceiving, etc.

COGNITIVE-BEHAVIORAL THERAPY (CBT) works to solve current problems and change unhelpful thinking and behavior. CBT combines behavioral therapy, which focuses on behaviors and the thoughts and feelings that cause them, and cognitive therapy, which helps individuals overcome difficulties by identifying and changing distorted thinking. CBT has been shown to have a role in the treatment of personality disorders, depression, schizophrenia, depression, and other psychiatric illnesses.

COMORBID means the presence of one or more additional disorders or diseases that co-occur with a primary disease or disorder. These medical conditions exist simultaneously and can be related or exist independently.

CUTTING is a form of self-injury or self-mutilation. The person is literally making small cuts on his or her body to help control emotional pain. The problem is particularly common among girls and often is a symptom for borderline personality disorder, as well as other psychiatric problems.

DEPRESSION is a mood disorder that causes a persistent feeling of sadness and loss of interest. It is often accompanied by difficulties with sleep and appetite.

DIAGNOSTIC AND STATISTICAL MANUAL, 5th EDITION is a system of classification of psychiatric diagnoses published in 2013.

DIAGNOSTIC CRITERIA are the clinical features that must be present to make a diagnosis of a mental disorder.

DIALECTICAL BEHAVIOR THERAPY (DBT) was developed by Dr. Marsha Linehan predominantly for the treatment of chronically suicidal BPD patients. Today it is the most widely used therapy for BPD, combining cognitive, behavioral, and Zen approaches to help people change patterns of behavior such as self-harm, suicidal thinking, and substance abuse. The treatment teaches specific skills to manage emotions, control impulsiveness, and diminish self-destructive behavior.

DISSOCIATION is an experience of having one's attention and emotions detached from reality.

DYSREGULATION is the inability to control or regulate one's mood. Possible manifestations are angry outbursts, throwing objects, aggression toward oneself or others, and threats to kill oneself.

EMOTION REGULATION DISORDER is the term that is preferred by clinicians over the term "borderline personality disorder" because it more accurately describes the illness and is not as stigmatizing or misleading as is the term "borderline personality disorder."

ETIOLOGY is the study of cause or origination.

FEAR OF ABANDONMENT is an irrational belief that one is in imminent danger of being personally rejected, discarded, or replaced.

IMPULSIVITY is the inability to resist performing an action.

INVALIDATION is a failure to legitimize the emotions, thoughts, or experiences of another. It is telling another that his or her feelings or perceptions are not real or don't matter.

LABILITY means rapid fluctuation or instability.

LIMBIC SYSTEM is a ring of interconnected structures in the middle of the brain. The limbic system is generally considered to be the emotional center of the brain, as it is in charge of regulating the expression of emotions, particularly fear and rage, both of which people with borderline personality disorder express in excess. Two of the limbic structures, the amygdale and the hippocampus, have been shown to be significantly smaller in people with BPD than in people who do not have any mental illness, indicating that there could be a link between BPD and a dysfunctional limbic system.

MHMRA is the Mental Health and Mental Retardation Authority of Houston. It provides care and support through three service divisions: Mental Health, Intellectual & Developmental Disabilities, and Comprehensive Psychiatric Emergency Programs.

MINDFULNESS is a key component of DBT, derived from Eastern Zen practices, that refers to being fully aware of one's moment-to-moment experiences. Mindfulness skills are the first skills taught in dialectical behavior therapy and are consistently repeated. The concept of mindful awareness originated in early Buddhist practice, but as taught in DBT is a non-religious, practical skills module focused on achieving a balance between emotionality and reasonable, rational thought.

MOMENT OF CLARITY are spontaneous, temporary periods when persons with a personality disorder are able to see beyond their own world view and can, for a brief period, understand, acknowledge, articulate and begin to make amends for their dysfunctional behavior.

MOOD is a long-lasting emotional state. Moods differ from emotions or feelings in that they are less specific, less intense, and less likely to be triggered.

MOOD STABILIZERS are psychiatric medications used to treat intense mood shifts and impulsive behaviors.

MOOD SWINGS are unpredictable, rapid, dramatic emotional cycles which cannot be readily explained by changes in external circumstances.

NEUROIMAGING, or brain imaging, has allowed significant findings concerning the brain and how it works. Scientists are studying differences in the brains of people with and without a mental illness to learn more about these disorders. However, at this time relying on brain scans alone cannot accurately diagnose a mental illness or tell you your risk of getting a mental illness in the future. Examples of brain imaging include computerized axial tomography (CAT scan), which uses a series of x-rays; magnetic resonance imaging (MRI), which uses radio waves and magnetic fields instead of radiation to obtain brain images; and positron emission tomography (PET scan), which measures emissions from radioactive chemicals that have been injected into the bloodstream.

NEUROLEPTIC MEDICATIONS are antipsychotic medications.

NEUROPSYCHOLOGY is the study of the relationship between neurons in the brain and psychological experiences such as thoughts, feelings, and perceptions.

NEUROSIS is a class of mental disorders involving chronic distress or anxiety but neither delusions nor hallucinations.

NEUROTRANSMITTERS are brain chemicals, such as serotonin, dopamine, nor epinephrine, and cortisol, which relay signals between nerve cells. Low levels of serotonin has been linked to the cause of borderline personality disorder. If the human body is running low on serotonin, a person can become severely depressed and angry, with tendencies to show aggression and act out. Low serotonin is also associated with suicide attempts. Dopamine and noradrenalin can also have the same effect as serotonin when the body is running low. People with BPD also have high levels of cortisol, a chemical released during stress. These high levels can predict a higher risk of suicide over time.

PARASUICIDAL refers to any self-injury, with or without suicidal intent, which does not result in death.

PERSONALITY DISORDERS are, according to the DSM-5, associated with one's way of thinking and feeling about oneself and others that significantly and adversely affects how an individual functions in many aspects of life.

PHARMACOTHERAPY is therapy using pharmaceutical drugs.

PRE-FRONTAL CORTEX is the front part of the brain behind the forehead and regulates the limbic system through the use of neurotransmitters. This brain region has also been implicated in planning complex cognitive behavior, personality expression, decision making, and moderating social behavior. The pre-frontal cortex is not as developed and has a lower level of activity in people with BPD than in people without it.

PROGNOSIS is a medical term for predicting the likely outcome of a condition, including the chance for relapse. A complete prognosis includes the expected duration, the function, and a description of the course of the disease.

PSYCHIATRIST is a medical doctor (M.D.) who specializes in preventing, diagnosing, and treating mental illness. A psychiatrist's training includes four years of medical school, one year of internship, and at least three years of psychiatric residency. As a doctor, a psychiatrist is licensed to write prescriptions.

PSYCHOLOGIST has a doctoral degree (Ph.D., Psy.D., or Ed.D.) in psychology, which is the study of the mind and behaviors. After completing graduate school, a psychologist completes an internship that lasts up to three years. Licensed psychologists are qualified to do counseling and psychotherapy, perform psychological testing, and provide treatment for mental disorders. They are not, however, medical doctors and thus cannot write prescriptions, except in only a handful of states. They generally work closely with a psychiatrist who provides the medical treatment for mental illness while the psychologist provides the psychotherapy.

PSYCHOSIS pertains to an abnormal condition of the mind and refers to a loss of contact with reality.

PSYCHOTHERAPY is the treatment of mental and emotional disorders through the use of psychological techniques designed to encourage communication of conflicts and insight into problems, with the goal being personality growth and behavior modification.

PSYCHOTROPIC MEDICATIONS are drugs that change brain function to alter behavior or experience.

RADICAL ACCEPTANCE is total acceptance of a person or situation, that you acknowledge reality for what it is, that you accept it from the depths of your soul. When you have radically accepted something, you stop fighting it and accept that life can be worth living even with painful events in it. It is a basic tenet of dialectical behavior therapy.

SELF-INJURIOUS BEHAVIOR is intentional, nonsuicidal self-injury, sometimes called self-mutilation, used in an attempt to mask emotional pain. Examples are cutting, burning, head banging, and hitting oneself.

SOCIAL WORKERS usually have master's degrees and are qualified to do psychotherapy.

SPLITTING is also called black-and-white thinking. It is a common defense mechanism where a person sees people as all good or all bad in order to control emotional turmoil. There is a failure in the person's thinking to bring together both positive and negative qualities of the self and others into a cohesive, realistic whole.

SUICIDAL IDEATION concerns thoughts about or an unusual preoccupation with committing suicide or taking one's life.

VALIDATION is empathizing with, or legitimizing the emotions, thoughts, and experiences of another. It is the recognition and acceptance of another person's thoughts, feelings, sensations, and behaviors as understandable. It does not require approval, just acceptance. Validation is a critical component in DBT, not only to help clients build their self-esteem, but to encourage their active participation throughout the therapeutic process.

About the Author

Linda Kana Burch is a retired college English professor who has degrees from The University of Texas at Austin and the University of Houston – Clear Lake. She lives in Houston, Texas, with her husband, Bill, and is the mother of two children, one with borderline personality disorder. She and her husband are trained instructors of the Family Connections course that was created by the National Education Alliance for Borderline Personality Disorder. They are also trained in suicide prevention, and they facilitate a support group for family members of borderlines. She is the author of *Growing Up Borderline: A Mother's Memoir*, which is the prequel to *Living Borderline*.

www.ingramcontent.com/pod-product-compliance
Lightning Source LLC
Chambersburg PA
CBHW051816090426
42736CB00011B/1504